GROWING A HEALTHY FAMILY

JIM LARSON

AUGSBURG Publishing House • Minneapolis

GROWING A HEALTHY FAMILY

Copyright © 1986 Augsburg Publishing House

Scripture quotations unless otherwise noted are from the Holy Bible: New International Version. Copyright 1978 by the New York International Bible Society. Used by permission of Zondervan Bible Publishers.

Library of Congress Cataloging-in-Publication Data

Larson, Jim, 1942–
  GROWING A HEALTHY FAMILY.

  Bibliography: p.
  1. Child rearing—Religious aspects—Christianity.
  2. Parenting—Religious aspects—Christianity.   3. Family
  —Religious life.   I. Title.
  HQ769.3.L37   1986   649'.1   85-28657
  ISBN 0-8066-2193-1

Manufactured in the U.S.A.   APH 10-2901

1   2   3   4   5   6   7   8   9   0   1   2   3   4   5   6   7   8   9

To my parents
with love and appreciation

Contents

Preface

Have you ever had a problem in your family that did not get resolved? No matter how much you talked or argued about it, the issue just got bigger and bigger, your resources for dealing with it seemed less and less, and you felt more and more frustrated and helpless.

Maybe you just feel stuck in your family. Nothing seems to go particularly good or bad. You just feel bored and disillusioned.

Maybe you feel as if you are living with a group of strangers in your family—little communication, even less happiness, only existing together under one roof.

Perhaps you are basically satisfied with what's been happening in your family, but you would like to know how to make your family life even better or more fulfilling.

Many people feel that something is just not right in their families, that there must be more than what they are experiencing.

If these have been your feelings, then this book has been written for you. Whether your feelings are rather vague ("I just can't seem to figure out why our family life always seems

a mess"), or more specific ("We have never learned to resolve our conflicts very well"), you've made an important
discovery that something may need to change in your family
relationships.

This book is not intended primarily to describe what goes
wrong in families or how families become unhealthy (although a section of the book does deal with this). Instead,
we will be focusing on what qualities mark healthy family
living, and how these qualities can be strengthened.

Every family—no matter how broken and unhealthy, or
how vibrant and healthy, has the potential for greater growth
and satisfaction. It is toward this end of living in healthy,
strong families that this book has been written.

PART ONE

SO WHAT'S THE DIFFERENCE?

1

Stressed to the Breaking Point

Everyone is gathered on the big front porch in the twilight of a warm summer evening, with grandma and grandpa slowly rocking in their chairs, mother bringing out a pitcher of cold lemonade, dad talking about the "good old days," the children enjoying themselves in obvious harmony. Later, everyone goes to bed at the same time, so that as the lights go out, we hear, "Good night, John-boy." "Good night, grandma." "Good night, Mary Ellen." "Good night, daddy."

Do families like that exist anymore? Maybe a better question is whether families like that *ever* existed!

Families have been undergoing major changes in recent years—changes that have resulted in many families feeling stressed to the breaking point. Let's look at some of these changes and stresses.

Explosion in Knowledge and Technology

Have you ever felt as if your child knows more than you do? You're not alone, and with our children taking courses in computer technology, electronics, and the like, there may be good reason for this feeling.

Did you know that three-fourths of the knowledge we have today was not known at the close of World War II? What is even more startling is that for children born in the 1970s, cumulative world knowledge will have quadrupled by the time they graduate from college. And when these people have reached age 50, 97% of everything known in the world will have been learned since they were born.

In *Future Shock* (Random House, 1970) Alvin Toffler provides us with a graphic example of how quickly change has taken place in our world. He says that if we divide the last 50,000 years of human existence into lifetimes of approximately 62 years each, there would have been about 800 such lifetimes. Of these, 650 were spent in caves. Only during the past 70 lifetimes have people been able to communicate effectively through writing. During the past six lifetimes we have seen the development of the printed word. And only during the past two lifetimes have we had electric motors. Most material goods we use daily have been developed within the present 800th lifetime.

No wonder some of us have developed feelings of future shock, which Toffler defines as "the dizzying disorientation brought on by the premature arrival of the future."

With this revolution in technology has come the impact of television. By age 16 a typical child will have watched 12,000 to 15,000 hours of television. By the time children become adults, most of them will have spent more time watching television than at school or in quality experiences with their families.

Revolution in Relationships

In recent years another revolution is having a great impact on families—that of changing roles and expectations in relationships. Discussion about the similarities and differences between males and females has been increasing. Many of the old generalizations (men should hide their feelings, women are the "weaker sex," and so on) have proven to be untrue.

But as we eliminate many of the old guidelines, we may find ourselves with no clear guidelines as to how to act in relationships. If men and women are truly equals, what does that mean for their relationships in terms of dating, making decisions, and expressing affection? For example, should women feel that it is acceptable for them to ask men out on dates or initiate expressions of affection? And how do all of these changes affect leadership in the home?

Pressures in Growing Up

There has also been increased pressure on children and young people to grow up faster and achieve more. Dr. David Elkind has said that there are many "hurried children" today, those who are pressured to become adults before their time. Clothing styles, hairstyles, and tastes in music are evidence of this pressure to grow up too soon.

Research by the Allan Guttmacher Institute indicates that, as part of this pressure to grow up faster, there is increased sexual activity for both young men and women. By age 19, four-fifths of the males and two-thirds of the females will have had sexual intercourse.

And with inadequate sexual and reproduction knowledge, approximately one-half of all births outside of marriage and one-third of abortions happen to teenage mothers. Even more startling is the Guttmacher Institute's prediction that four of every ten girls who are now 14 years old will become pregnant at least once during their adolescent years.

Struggles with Questions of Morality

With all these changes and transitions come many new moral questions with which we are forced to struggle. There is concern about whether there is life after death, and when life begins and ends. Families may find themselves confronted with the reality of an unwanted teenage pregnancy. Painful choices are involved when thinking of whether to keep the baby, give it up for adoption, or consider an abortion.

A group of sixth-grade children recently reminded me of the complexities of another issue. They arrived at Sunday school with an urgent question: whether or not euthanasia (mercy killing) was an acceptable alternative for Christians. Their opinions and insights revealed a serious concern for issues with which I did not have to deal until I was an adult.

The Family as Giant Shock Absorber

Toffler notes that traditionally the family has been society's "giant shock absorber"—the place to which people return after days filled with frustration and conflict. For many the family has remained a stable anchor in a stormy sea of change.

But all these recent changes and issues have created great stresses. Many families have been stretched to the breaking point, and there is mounting evidence that family stresses are being expressed in hurtful ways. Here are a few indications of how serious the situation has become.

• Child abuse has become an epidemic problem in our society. At least one million children are being abused or neglected annually, with reports of an increase of 30% per year.

• This epidemic of violence is also seen in relationships between spouses. In one out of every six marriages, beatings are commonplace. Even more alarming is an FBI report showing that family conflicts account for one-fourth of all murders in our society.

• An increasing number of people are turning their stresses inward on themselves rather than outwards in violence. Among adolescent young people, for example, suicide has become the second most frequent cause of death (after auto accidents). The rate of suicides among both children and youth has increased dramatically in recent years.

My wife Jill and I have been piloting a course for children, called "Kids Can Cope Creatively," in which children learn to deal with their feelings and to manage stress at school and at home. The children take a written test in which a number of stressful events and changes (both positive and negative) are listed. Each event has a numerical score, according to how stressful it is considered to be. After the events are checked, each child is given a total score regarding the stress experienced during the past year. A score of 300 or more indicates severe stress. We were shocked to find that more than half the children had scores of over 300 and that several children scored over 500.

No Wonder!

Perhaps it is no wonder that many people and families today are feeling burned out, tired, frustrated, confused, unsure, afraid, like giving up.

One of the unusual things about stress is that it can be both a cause and an effect of changes within and outside of our families. As we are faced by new knowledge and other changes, we may feel pressured to adapt and change; as we grow in our family relationships, such changes can also cause stress.

If you are one who feels discouraged about what is happening in your family, remember that the purpose of this book is to give you hope for change and for growing health, as well as specific ideas on how your family relationships can become healthier and stronger.

Next Steps

1. Reflect on what life was like for you as a child. In what ways is life more stressful and complex for your children than it was for you in your early years? In what ways was it more difficult for you?

2. Reflect on the changes affecting families as they were described in this chapter. Which of these changes has had the greatest influence on your family? In what ways have these changes been positive? negative?

2

One-of-a-Kind Families

For many years, one of the favorite television programs for children was *Mr. Rogers' Neighborhood,* which contributed a great deal to the self-esteem and well-being of children. In his own quiet way, Mr. Rogers said to children: "You are so special. There is no one in the world just like you. You're one of a kind, so enjoy it!"

How healthy it is to realize that each person is one of a kind—unique and special! We are so special that children of the same parents may have any of 250 billion different chromosome combinations. If you had brothers or sisters as you were growing up, you know that you were like them in some ways, but quite different in others. Your looks are unique. Your moods, feelings, and temperaments may be quite different from those around you. Even your values may be different.

Your Family Is One of a Kind

Just as we are all unique individuals, so our families are different from each other. Each family has a special "personality" that develops over the lifetime of a family—a dynamic that is revealed in how people communicate, handle their feelings and conflicts, and behave according to their values.

Families may look like each other in some ways, but even on the outside—what others usually see—we are different. Some families have two parents; others have one. Some include grandparents and other relatives living together or nearby, while others are estranged or separated from their extended families. Still others involve a remarriage.

And inside the family, in the dynamic of family functioning, the uniqueness of each family unit is most clearly observed. For example, some families handle their feelings quite openly and frankly, while others are more indirect. Some even deny that feelings such as anger exist and repress them.

Some families handle their conflicts by reaching for consensus or common agreement whenever possible. Others designate some family members (usually the parents, but not always) to make the decisions for everyone. Other families rarely resolve conflicts. They tend to get "stuck" over the most trivial issues, as well as the more significant ones.

Some families value traditions and heritage, while others feel cut off or on their own, with few family ties. Some families thus feel quite close, while others seem quite estranged from one another.

Some families place greatest value on togetherness, others focus on individuality, and still others blend the two.

Some families really enjoy one another and look forward to family times of playing and sharing, while in other families persons merely tolerate one another.

Each family has a unique personality, a pattern that often becomes set and predictable. And since all families are unique, some of them develop patterns that are quite healthy, while others become quite unhealthy and dysfunctional.

Exactly why this happens is a mystery. It may have to do with the models and examples we had in our families of origin as we were growing up. Our values and needs also affect our family patterns. And the dynamic created among the family members certainly makes a difference.

Whatever the causes, we can look at these dynamics and evaluate how we are doing. We can choose to work on the quality of our family relationships. We do not have to remain in dysfunctional or unhappy patterns.

But what are the indicators that tell us how our families are doing? Let's meet two families to find out what their relationships are like.

Family #1

Bill and Ginny have been married for 21 years. They have three children: a daughter Laura, who is about to graduate from high school; a daughter Tina, just entering junior high school; and a son Bill Jr., who is in fifth grade.

From all outward appearances, this family is healthy and happy. Bill was just promoted to regional sales manager of his company. Ginny runs a boutique, where the children help out part-time. The family looks well-groomed and happy—the "perfect" family, you may think.

But let's enter their household as they are about to eat dinner.

Ginny calls, "Dinner's ready, it's on your plates." She is met only by silence. She yells, "I said dinner's ready!"

One at a time, family members straggle into the kitchen, pick up a plate of food, and return to the den. They eat in silence, continuing to watch television. The only conversation revolves around what program to watch. After dinner Laura returns to her room and spends the evening talking on the phone to friends. Tina and Bill Jr. continue watching television until bedtime. Bill works on papers for the next day's meeting, and Ginny works on the books for her business.

"What's wrong with that?" you may ask. Probably most families have evenings like that. True, but for family #1, this is the pattern every night of the week, as well as for every weekend. They are together physically, but they are not really together. They rarely share. There is no closeness. Most of the communication takes place through blank stares, turns of the head, and shrugs of the shoulders.

For this family, problems don't get resolved. They just get pushed aside and ignored. As a result, there is no deep sharing of feelings. In fact, when they're being honest, the family members admit that they don't really feel like a family. They are like five individuals who just happen to live under the same roof, like guests at a hotel.

It is not that life is bad. They have almost anything that money can buy, and they are financially secure. But the family members do not know how to relate to one another, and they really don't know one another.

Family #2

Bob and Julie have been married for 13 years. They have a son Charles, who is in sixth grade. Bob owns his own plumbing business, while Julie is a homemaker.

Charles has recently started having trouble at school. He is not turning in homework, even when he has completed the work. He sits quietly in class and stares out the window.

Charles has just arrived home with his report card, which describes his less-than-average grades. Let's listen in:

Julie: Charles, did you bring home your report card? (*No response.*) Charles, I'm talking to you! Where's your report card?

Charles: I-it-it's right here. (*He hands his mother a wadded-up piece of paper. Julie flattens it out, looks at it, and gasps.*)
Julie: This is terrible! You're just like your father! You'll never amount to anything. How could you be so stupid?
Bob (*entering the room*): What's all the ruckus?
Julie (*handing the report card to Bob*): Look how stupid our son is! He's just as dumb as you!
Bob: Now, wait a minute! I may not be the world's smartest person, but you're no Einstein yourself. You can't even hold down a job!
Julie: Yes, I can. I quit my last job because we had Charlie. That's the worst mistake I ever made.
Bob: You're just like your mother! You can never make up your mind. You're just fickle!
Julie: Well, at least I try. All you do is sit home at night and watch television and read the paper. We haven't gone out for months.

Bob picks up a dish and throws it down on the floor with a resounding crash. Julie runs into her bedroom crying and slams the door. Bob walks out of the front door, slamming it as he goes. And Charles stands alone in the kitchen, staring at the wadded-up report card, wondering what happened.

What really did happen?

This family turns almost every conflict into a battle. No matter how minor the concern, someone always manages to use it as a weapon to attack the other family members. Every issue becomes a major war.

Thus far tempers have eventually cooled down. After all the yells, screams, accusations, and slammed doors, there is usually a period of stony silence, then limited communication, and finally a return to "business as usual."

But the downward spiral in family closeness continues.

Each confrontation becomes a little more vicious, a little more abusive, and a lot more personal.

No wonder that Charles struggles with his self-esteem and his ability to function at school. For as long as he can remember, he has been called "slow," "stupid," "dumb," and "a failure." More and more, Charles is living up—or *down*—to these labels.

Family #2 remains in trouble, because they have not learned how to communicate effectively. Their negative patterns have stifled the positive feelings that can exist in a family. Both partners find themselves wishing that they could end all this misery, but at this point, they have not figured out how.

It Doesn't Have to Be Like This!

For some families life may not be too bad. They do not experience stresses or conflicts, but there is great emotional distance, a sense of estrangement, among family members.

For others there is a great deal of conflict, open and direct, or hidden and indirect. Either way, family members live in fear as they anticipate the next volcanic eruption.

In still other families, there seems to be a great deal of contentment and fulfillment. They seem genuinely to enjoy each other.

Then, too, it's not as if most families are all terrible or all wonderful. Most families are somewhere in the middle.

And families experience fluctuations in their relationships. Just as individuals experience times of stability and times of transition, uncertainty, and stress, so do families. Adjustments to outward circumstances (like economic stresses and job changes), and inner dynamics (such as the birth of a child, a child leaving home, and so on) can affect the family's effort to keep itself balanced and functioning.

But regardless of circumstances and the quality of our family relationships, there is always room for growing and changing, for discovering and building on the strengths that can enhance togetherness and fulfillment. Several important steps need to be taken: (1) understanding what healthy families are like, (2) evaluating the health of one's own family, (3) deciding what changes need to take place, (4) acting on these decisions, and (5) evaluating whether or not the changes have been effective.

Next Steps

1. Think back to the family in which you grew up. Visualize a place where you lived. Think of what it was like when family members were together.

- What are some of your positive memories?
- What are some memories you'd just as soon forget?
- If you came from a two-parent family, how would you describe the quality of your parents' marriage?
- Did family members seem close or estranged?
- How were conflicts handled?
- What were some of the good times your family had?
- What were some of the points of crisis, transition, or stress? How did your family handle such times?

2. In getting in touch with these feelings and memories, you may want to keep a journal for the next few weeks. Write down your reflections and feelings as frankly and specifically as you can. Then review your notes and see what you discover from your reflections.

Remember: unless we choose to do otherwise, we tend to repeat patterns from our families of origin, whether these patterns are positive and healthy, or negative and unhealthy. Taking steps to grow begins by taking an honest look at patterns from our families of origin to see whether or not they are influencing our families today.

3

What Healthy Families Are Like

Health is more than the absence of illness. A physically healthy person is not only one who rarely gets sick, but a person who has energy, zest, and is generally happy. Such a person *feels* well—a feeling that is often evidenced by a healthy glow.

Emotional health, too, is more than the absence of emotional dysfunctions, such as deep depression or neurosis. To be emotionally healthy is to feel happy and successful about life. In *Pathfinders* (Bantam, 1981) Gail Sheehy identifies these qualities of the emotionally healthy person:

- life has meaning and direction;
- one or more transitions in adult life have been experienced and handled in an unusual, personal, or creative way;
- feelings of being cheated or disappointed rarely exist;
- several long-term goals have already been attained;
- progress in personal growth and development has brought feelings of pleasure;
- being able to both give and receive love is apparent;

- there are many friends;
- there is cheerfulness;
- there is little sensitivity to criticism;
- there are no major fears.

Admittedly, most people are still "in process" in one or more of these areas, but these seem to be worthy goals that contribute to well-being.

For a life-style of wellness, then, the goal is not only to reduce the incidence of illness or disease, but to find greater meaning, purpose, and deeper satisfaction in living.

Health in Families

Healthy families are like that. Not only do they show no evidence of severe dysfunctions in their relationships, but they have an energy, a zest, an enthusiasm and happiness that is often apparent, if not contagious, to others around them. Healthy families show a closeness that is easy to admire.

For decades research has been done on the causes and effects of family dysfunction or disease. My shelves are full of books on various family problems and how they should be handled. But, until recently, little has been written on family health and how it can be enhanced. Happily, this trend has begun to change, with a developing literature regarding family health and strengths (see For Further Reading).

Some fascinating research is being conducted by Dr. Nick Stinnett and his associates. In *Family Strengths: Positive Models for Family Life* (University of Nebraska Press, 1980) Dr. Stinnett defines family strengths as those relationship patterns, interpersonal skills and competencies, and social and psychological characteristics which create a sense of positive family identity, promote satisfying and fulfilling interaction among family members, encourage the development of the potential of the family group and individual family members, and contribute to the family's ability to deal effectively with stress and crises.

Notice that Dr. Stinnett describes family strengths as patterns, skills, and competencies. These aspects of family relationships do not necessarily come naturally, any more than a person knows how to type or drive a car without developing the necessary skills. Any skill worth having usually takes a great deal of practice, whether it's playing the piano, throwing a football, ballet dancing, or public speaking. These strengths in family life are also skills that can be developed through hard work and practice.

Dr. Stinnett implies that family strengths are more than the absence of severe family problems. He mentions several values of these strengths:

● *They create a sense of positive family identity.* People enjoy belonging to families where there is health.

● *They promote satisfying and fulfilling interaction among family members.* The communication patterns in healthy families bring satisfaction and enjoyment. Such persons are able to move beyond shouting matches and put-downs to communicate in ways that are both truthful and loving.

● *They encourage the growth of the family as a unit, as well as of each individual person in it.* To be a member of a healthy family does not mean that a person has to give up personal growth or goals. Instead, there is encouragement to fulfill one's potential as a human being. Such personal growth in each member creates a climate of health for the whole family.

● *They help the family to deal effectively with stress and conflicts.* When faced with crises or conflict, healthy families don't seem to get stuck for long. They have developed the necessary skills to resolve the conflicts and to move on in life.

Family Strengths

Dr. Stinnett and other researchers have discovered that healthy families seem to share several important characteristics. Let's look briefly at each of these family strengths.

1. Commitment
Commitment is a bond that holds a family together, even during times of crisis, difficulty, or change. Healthy families have a feeling of mutual trust, a shared sense of responsibility in which each family member feels involved.

Family relationships are valued. This can be seen in family traditions and times of celebration or commemoration that have special meaning for the family.

2. Time
Time together is an important priority in the healthy family, both in terms of quality and quantity. Despite the pressures that can drive family members apart, healthy families often share such moments as mealtimes, as well as leisure times, together.

3. Appreciation
Healthy families appreciate each of their members. There is a supportive, affirming environment in which persons express their love for each other in specific, meaningful ways.

Persons in healthy families usually feel loved and appreciated, and thus feel free to express their love to other family members as well.

4. Communication

Communication in the healthy family is direct, loving, and constructive. Persons take responsibility for expressing their feelings but also work hard at listening to the feelings and needs of the others.

People in healthy families are learning to say what they mean and mean what they say. The communications of each person are valued and accepted, even if there is a difference of opinion.

5. Conflict Resolution

The goal in healthy families is not to avoid crisis or pain, but to deal with difficulties in positive and constructive ways.

The approach to conflicts or crises is one of flexibility and adaptability. Creative resolutions for conflicts are sought, and rules for dealing with conflict are both realistic and clear.

In healthy families conflicts do get resolved. They are not avoided or repressed, but are faced with a desire to get them resolved.

Healthy families get stronger as a result of dealing with the conflicts and crises of life. Even when it is stretched by difficulties, their bond of togetherness becomes stronger and more durable in coping with the realities of life.

6. Faith

Healthy families share a solid core of moral and spiritual beliefs. There is concern about the rightness and wrongness of actions, as well as for how actions will affect other people.

In healthy families a belief in God and a desire to love and serve God is an important value. Even if there is a difference of opinion regarding specific religious beliefs and practices, the spiritual part of life is appreciated. The development of a relationship with God is encouraged and supported.

Healthy families, then, do not become emotional or relational islands, trying to cope with life without the support of anyone else. Instead, healthy families realize that they need the encouragement and support of others, including the strength and meaning that comes from a life of faith.

A Word of Caution and Reassurance

Each of these strengths is not an absolute—something a family either has or does not have. They exist on a sliding scale—from absolutely perfect to absolutely lacking. Most families probably have a measure of some of these strengths.

One family, for example, may have a strong sense of commitment but lack the communication or conflict-resolution skills that could make their life less stressful.

Another family may have a strong bond of faith but lack the necessary quality time in which its relationships could be nurtured and strengthened.

Each family has a unique balance of these qualities, just as each of us is a unique person with special gifts, abilities, strengths, and limitations.

No matter how strong or healthy our families are, we all have growing edges—those areas that need to have our attention so that our families can become even stronger and healthier.

Next Steps

1. Think about each of these six strengths in your own family relationship. On each continuum on the next page, place an X where you think your family would score. Afterwards, total the numbers from each of the six family strengths. (Lowest possible score is 6, highest is 30.)

	Not yet begun	Just started	About half-way there	Mostly developed	Totally developed
	1	2	3	4	5
1. Strong commitment					
2. Family time a priority					
3. Expressions of appreciation in evidence					
4. Healthy communication					
5. Effective conflict resolution skills					
6. Common bond of faith					

2. Take a few moments to reflect on your score. Identify which one (or more) of the family strengths most needs your attention. You may want to read first the chapters in the next section that deal with your greatest concerns. Then read the other chapters as well, because all families have potential for growth in all of these areas.

PART TWO

RECIPE FOR A HEALTHY FAMILY

4

Commitment

The family life cycle typically starts with the marriage of two persons. And the marriage usually begins with a wedding ceremony in which the persons commit themselves to live in a relationship that is healthy and loving.

A traditional wedding ceremony often contains the following words:

I, _____ , take thee, _____ , to be my wedded wife/husband; And I do promise and covenant before God and these witnesses to be thy loving and faithful husband/wife, in plenty and in want, in joy and in sorrow, in sickness and in health, As long as we both shall live.

A more contemporary ceremony might contain vows like this:

_____ , I take you as my wife/husband; and I promise before God and our friends that I will love you to the best of my ability. I will comfort you, honor and respect you, in sickness and in health; when our joy is deep, and when tears come; when we are together, or alone. I will strive to be worthy of your love, as we change and grow together.

Often a wedding ceremony includes the giving and receiving of rings as a symbol of the commitment that is being made.

How unfortunate that no such commitment is required or expected when a couple chooses to have a child. The only requirement is the physical ability to get pregnant and carry the child full-term. For many people, becoming a biological parent is rather easy; learning to become a nurturing, loving parent takes many of us a number of years.

It is true that some kind of commitment ceremony is provided by many religions in the form of Baptism or dedication. Most of these ceremonies involve a commitment on the part of the parents to bring up the child in a responsible way; they also involve a commitment on the part of a congregation to provide the support and examples that are essential for people to grow up to be healthy persons. Yet many people have children and do not think fully of what will be involved in helping them to grow to maturity.

Perhaps we need some kind of commitment ceremony soon after the child's birth. The vows might read something like this:

_____ , I promise to commit my energies and resources to be the kind of parent you need me to be: loving, concerned, nurturing, and consistent. I promise to stay committed to our relationship during the rough times, as well as the good times; during the transitions and adjustments, as well as during more predictable periods. Even when you feel like leaving, I will love and respect you. I will work to become more flexible and to develop the skills I will need to be a healthy parent. I look forward to all you will become, as well as to what our relationship will help me become.

What Is Commitment?

According to Webster, to commit is to bind oneself, to pledge; it is to involve in risk, to agree to be related. Commitment is the glue that holds families together through both happy and difficult times. It is the choice to stay involved and in relationship, even during times when that relationship is in crisis or transition.

Commitment transcends feelings of closeness. Certainly times of feeling close or intimate are essential for both marriage and family life. But with the realities of life, with all the stresses and changes we encounter, such feelings cannot stay constant. As important as feelings are as a monitor of our deepest needs, values, and reactions, they can also be quite fickle, because they are influenced by physical well-being, stress levels, fatigue, and outward circumstances.

Commitment may need to become "true grit," a "hanging in" with someone when the commitment does not seem to be reciprocated. It may also be the choice of saying no when we sense that we are being abused or manipulated, as we will see later in this chapter.

Throughout the life cycle of the healthy family, commitment will continue to grow and become strong. Commitment could be compared to a muscle that will become stronger and more useful through frequent use. Commitment grows and develops as family members encounter each other, share their needs, deal with conflicts, and seek to strengthen their relationships. A strong, vibrant commitment will guide a healthy family through the most difficult and unpredictable times.

What Is Weak Commitment Like?

A family with weak commitment is one in which both parents and children threaten separation or ending the relationship, especially when there are conflicts or disappointments.

Weak commitments begin early in the life of the family with such comments as the following:

"Daddy doesn't like children who spill their milk."

"Mommy doesn't love boys who cry."

"I won't love you anymore if you don't do what I say."

Such comments make children assume that the parent's love for them is based on the children's *actions*, not on *who they are*. Families with weak commitment often use manipulation and threats.

A weak commitment may result in a temporary or permanent separation. For example, in college I knew a young man who was struggling with his course work. He could barely get B's and C's; A's seemed out of the question, no matter how hard he tried. His frustration was compounded by a threat he had received from his father early in his freshman year: if he didn't get mostly A's, he was not welcome to come home for Christmas vacation. Needless to say, this young man did not spend the holidays with his family, and the sense of alienation grew until the separation became permanent. The message he had heard for years was that he would be loved only if he were an outstanding student; average students were not worthy of their parents' love.

I remember a young woman who early in her teenage years became pregnant. Her boyfriend refused to marry her. Her parents literally threw her out of their house, and she had no place to go. She was faced with the dilemma of whether to get an abortion, carry the fetus full-term and then keep the child, or give it up for adoption.

She decided to keep the child, primarily because she had lost her family of origin and she thought this would be a way to develop a new family. Unfortunately, she was immature and needy herself and proved to be an unfit mother. More than once her baby was taken away by the courts as she struggled to get her life together. Even worse, her family refused to have any contact with her during this entire crisis.

Another couple was faced with a dilemma. They had fallen in love and wanted to get married, but the parents of the young man did not accept the young woman and refused to attend their wedding. In fact, the parents disinherited their son, because he did not marry someone who in their opinion was "good enough" for him. So, the marriage got off to a difficult start, and this lack of parental support became a point of contention for many years to come.

In some situations commitment is *conditional* ("I will love you if . . .") or *circumstantial* ("I will love you when . . ."). Unfortunately, such commitment tends to change erratically during the life cycle of the family—from its earliest days until the children have grown up and become adults.

How Is Strong Commitment Evidenced?

In these examples of weak commitment, one of the missing factors is trust, the quality that reveals acceptance of the integrity and worth of another person. Trust shows a willingness to be open and vulnerable with others, so that weaknesses and needs as well as strengths are revealed.

Trust is something that develops from the earliest days of life. In fact, according to researcher Erik Erikson, developing trust is an essential step in the first two years of life, necessary in becoming a healthy, fully functioning adult. If we do not develop trust in those early years, we tend to draw back from people, to feel insecure about whether or not we can count on those people to be reliable and trustworthy.

If we cannot trust other people, we cannot really be committed in relationships. Lack of trust shows itself in insecurity, self-doubts, and focusing on the other person's weaknesses and failures.

A developing trust, on the other hand, is not based just on feelings, which can fluctuate. Instead, trust is based on choice, a willingness to risk, to renew a relationship on a daily basis, to say yes to the person and relationship.

Commitment is also built on a developing and deepening feeling of togetherness, a quality based on the statement, "We belong together and to one another. No matter what comes, we are family." Such togetherness builds a bond of security that helps family members feel that they are accepted and loved, no matter what mistakes they make.

Such togetherness is not like a clinging vine that seeks to hang on to others, choking off their growth and independence. Instead, a positive, mature attitude helps us know when to let go and encourage independence, and when to hold on and encourage closeness and interdependence.

When we tell someone that we trust them and appreciate our togetherness, we are saying, "I value you. You are important to me. I am glad we are a family."

Such affirmation requires more than words, for without actions, such words can appear to be phony and syrupy. Belonging and togetherness are expressed through affection, both verbal and physical. The giving, as well as receiving, of such strokes greatly strengthens the bond of love that can exist in families. Our outward actions need to reinforce and reflect our inner feelings and commitments.

But What If Our Commitment Is Not Reciprocated?

At times in the life of every family, parents feel that the commitment they have for their children is not reciprocated, that their offspring do not care for them in the same manner or degree to which they feel committed. Perhaps the parents even feel taken advantage of at times.

This unequal commitment may cause some parents to feel like withdrawing from their children. They may stop communicating directly as a way to pay the children back for alleged disappointments and failures.

Or, in the case of a family with strong-willed adolescents, parents may feel the need to placate or give in to their children as a way of showing their love. Such families often become either dominated by the children or estranged, with family members being out of touch with one another.

Both extremes do not represent healthy family functioning. What is sometimes needed is "tough love." As we find ourselves dealing with conflicting values, we need to reassure our children of our commitment to and love for them, but we also need to set limits. Most young people do not flourish in homes where there are no rules or limits.

Setting limits and being consistent about them is a challenge. In the midst of being barraged by an angry teenager, we may feel like giving up or giving in—only to retreat into ourselves and live with a feeling of resentment and helplessness.

Staying close to family members who do not want to be close to us is one of the greatest challenges of parenting. And, in fact, a relationship can develop only so far as both persons want it to develop. At the same time, we must be careful not to let our commitment be based on the response we get from our children. To allow our commitment to fluctuate like the scale that measures earthquakes is to have strings attached to our love.

Especially with teenagers I have found that occasional and short-term separations can be helpful when tempers are flaring too often and conflicts do not seem to get resolved. We can all profit from a few days of rest from the intensive efforts we may be making to keep our families intact and on a healthy course.

I have often suggested to churches, schools, and other groups that we need to implement a plan of "rotational families" for our children. I have found that when a teenager lives with another family for a weekend or week, family members often have a greater appreciation for each other afterwards. If for no other reason, there is value in having an occasional break from one another.

The Ebb and Flow of Commitment

Commitment, then, is not a quality of family life that develops naturally and evenly through the life cycle. Instead, it tends to have an ebb and flow, just like the tides.

At times our commitment to other family members may seem strong, secure, as if nothing could affect it. I feel closest to my family when they ask me for help or show their love for me.

It is a great challenge for me to feel committed when I seem to feel unneeded, criticized, or neglected. Yet that is precisely when my commitment to my wife and children is most challenged and consequently can grow. We do not always grow in commitment when everything goes well. Despite the comfort and joy which such good times can bring, we probably grow strongest in our family relationships during times of transition, uncertainty, and change.

Such seasons of life can provide a good measurement of our trust and commitment.

If we find ourselves committed and trusting only when we receive these feelings of comfort and joy from the other family members, our commitment is *conditional* and *situational*. Then we need to build a commitment that can transcend or overcome those difficult times, which can cause such pain or tear us to emotional shreds.

Sometimes, our commitment may cause us to let go of a person, realizing that our efforts to stay close and in touch seem to be counterproductive. No matter how hard we try, there seems to be a widening chasm in the relationship. Or perhaps the other person has become so abusive or rejecting that no effort seems effective. At such times for our own well-being or safety, as well as for other family members, we may have to temporarily call a halt to further efforts. In many families such circumstances may never occur. Yet for other families, such steps may be essential.

When a family begins its earliest years together with a strong commitment and trust, a bond can develop which helps families enjoy their togetherness while encouraging independence and personal growth. This "thermometer" we call commitment is an essential measure of how healthy our family relationships seem to be.

Next Steps

1. Reflect on your family of origin. How would you describe the level of commitment with your parents and other family members? Were there any times when the level of commitment seemed to change significantly? What happened? How was family commitment (or lack of it) evidenced? How did your earliest experiences of trust and commitment affect the person and parent you have become?

2. Reflect on the strength or quality of commitment in your family today. Does it seem conditional, growing, or nonexistent? Do you find yourself wanting to be closer to the other family members? Do you find yourself thinking of ways to get away from your family? Or do you wish you could find ways to strengthen your family relationships?

3. On a sheet of paper draw a circle to represent every member of your family. Draw the size of the circles to show the level of commitment you think they have to your family relationship. Draw lines to show the depth or strength of various family relationships (thick lines for strong relationships, dotted lines for distant relationships, curvy lines to show an "up-and-down" relationship).

What do each of these diagrams show about the families and their commitment levels?

FAMILY A   **FAMILY B**

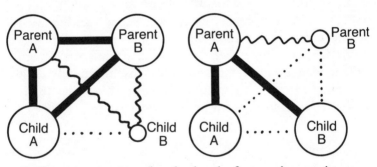

Reflect on reasons why the level of commitment in your family varies from person to person. Is it based on their personalities and temperaments? Where is each person in the life cycle (for example, entering adolescence, leaving home, midlife transition)? What are evidences that the commitment level is strong? weak? What can you plan to do to enhance your commitment to family members?

5

Time

Have you ever heard yourself saying things like, "I don't have time right now. I'll try to help you with your homework later," or, "I'm running out of time. Will you finish the dishes for me, so I can get to my meeting?" or, "Let's find a time to do something special. This is already a packed week," or perhaps, "Mark, please clean up your room. No wonder you can't find anything in it!"

Time—in many ways as precious as gold or silver. There never seems to be enough time to get everything done. There are the everyday tasks of managing a home—the cooking, washing, cleaning, and bookkeeping. There are the special tasks involved with crises or emergencies, such as a child's illness or accident, problems with relatives, or neighborhood concerns. There are jobs and other involvements outside the home.

All of these pressures can make us feel as if we are being squeezed in a steel vice. At times we may feel like giving up or running away. Sometimes life just gets too complicated.

Like silver or gold, time can be hoarded, spent, or shared. Time is something we can measure in seconds, minutes, hours, days, weeks, and years. Consequently, our use of time is an accurate indicator of our true values, more accurate than the words we speak. Time is a measure of our commitments.

How often I hear a parent say, "Family relationships are so important to me." I respond by asking to see their calendars—the most readily available guide to their use of time, and thus to their values regarding family life.

Time and Job Pressures

Among the many challenges to the effective use of time, one of the biggest is *jobs*. Let's look at a few people who struggle with the time their jobs consume.

Joe is a marketing representative for several corporations. He has to work away from home for weeks at a time. Because he is so rarely at home, most of his discussions regarding important family decisions take place by telephone.

Joe sees that his wife is becoming estranged from him, and that the children rarely consult him or share what is happening in their lives. To compound the difficulty, Joe finds that when he is finally at home, he is so exhausted from the pace of life on the road that he is not ready for family interaction—but only for reading, watching television, and sleeping.

Even though Joe is aware of this conflict between home and job, he feels helpless to do much about it, short of quitting this kind of work. And just when he feels that he is getting the job under control, one of the companies has asked him to do another "emergency" job that will involve enormous amounts of his energy and time.

Joe's identity has become so wrapped up in his work that he sees no practical way to change what is happening.

Lisa is the mother of a three-year-old child. She values family relationships and wants to spend time with her daughter. She has organized her job into three 12-hour days, so that she can spend two weekdays at home with her child.

But the price she is paying for the long, stressful days of her work as a stockbroker is enormous. She is constantly plagued by colds, flus, and other assorted ailments. By the time Thursday comes, she is so exhausted from her workdays that she needs one day to sleep in and recuperate from the previous three days.

Lisa is frazzled, and she does not know what to do about it. If she quits her job, her family will suffer severe financial difficulties. But she does not feel good about having her daughter in day care five days a week. She feels caught in this painful vice of where to spend her time and energies.

Jack has another kind of problem. He feels locked into a job that he finds boring and unfulfilling. He has been working in the same department in the same corporation for many years, and he has reached the peak of his earnings. Jack feels that he cannot afford to quit and look for another kind of work. With his three children in college and other expenses, Jack feels that he needs to stay with the job for another 15 years until he can finally retire.

In the meantime Jack feels trapped. Some mornings he even becomes physically ill. During the past year Jack has experienced more and more illnesses, and now he is beginning to have frequent migraine headaches.

When Jack is not at work, he feels as if he has been released from prison. He has involved himself in a number of hobbies and activities. In fact, Jack is rarely home during the evenings or on weekends. He seems to be trying to erase the pain of where he spends his best waking hours by becoming overinvolved in more fulfilling activities at other times.

As a result, Jack's wife Jan is frustrated by the lack of his attention. Not only has their last child gone off to college, but now she feels that she has lost her husband as well. Her complaint is one heard by so many, "We just never seem to have enough *time* to be together."

Jack reminds us of another important thought regarding our use of time. Some people do not invest their most creative energies in work—either because they work in jobs that are boring or repetitious, or because earning money is their only job goal. They do not find fulfillment in their job, so they become highly involved in activities during the off-work hours. Some people move on the time pendulum from being "workaholics" to becoming "funaholics" or "hobbyaholics." But the result is the same: a lack of time and energy for building healthy family relationships.

Time and Temperament

Your basic temperament also influences your use of time. Some people are by nature more task-oriented; they cannot relax until all of the work is done. I have heard parents say, "I can't sit down and be with my family until the whole house is picked up. I would be too uptight knowing that I would have to do the tasks later."

The problem that many task-oriented people face is that often the tasks just never seem to get done. As children continue to grow, the piles of dirty laundry, the scattered newspapers, and the toys that are not picked up just seem to get higher and higher. Finally, task-oriented persons are tyrannized by these tasks and either give up in despair, feeling like failures, or continue digging through the piles while family relationships get neglected.

An important goal in developing healthy families, then, is to work to become more person-oriented, to realize the value and fulfillment that come through involvement with our families in activities that are either serious or fun.

For many of us, this involves making difficult, at times "no-win," choices. When we are faced with a choice between survival and healthier family relationships, survival will win out. Abraham Maslow pointed that out when he devised what he called "the hierarchy of needs." Maslow maintained that there are certain basic survival needs, such as the needs for food, water, and air. The "higher" needs, such as the need for self-esteem, are essential for becoming what he calls a "self-actualized" (fully functioning, mature) person. But when there is a conflict between the survival and the esteem needs, the survival needs will always win out.

So I am not talking about quitting our jobs irresponsibly so that we can stay home with our children. Our responsibilities to provide financially for our families are certainly important. But there are times when the choice is not between survival and healthy family relationships, but between more equal alternatives. As we make healthy family functioning a priority, we may find ways to trim our outside involvements and commit some of our time to strengthening family relationships.

Quality Time

There is much talk today about the importance of *quality* time—those moments when undivided attention is paid to other persons, when the conversation is deep and open, when the feelings of togetherness and affection are apparent and spontaneously expressed.

In many families there are few such quality moments. One study of families with newborns found that the typical father spent only three to four minutes of quality time each day with his newborn child.

The situation is not much better for families where one of the parents chooses to stay at home (either instead of a career outside the home, or working on a career at home). Studies indicate that some parents tend to be near their children geographically (inside the same house, for example), but not necessarily be involved with them relationally at any deeper level than the parent who is away working all day.

To some people, having quality time together sounds serious and long faced, like sitting through a boring lecture. But quality time is often best experienced in moments of relaxation and fun. Sometimes a day trip to a lake or the mountains—just getting away from the everyday routine and familiar surroundings—can do wonders for feelings of family togetherness. Such outings need not cost a great deal. With a little thought and ingenuity, families can find many things to do—both at home and away—that can provide those quality moments together.

One of the hurdles we face with quality time is that it really cannot be structured to perfection. Most of us would not say to our children, "OK, kids, we need some quality time. Let's all sit down and be close!" Most children (as well as many parents) would feel that such an effort would be stilted and artificial.

Quality moments are often unexpected, unplanned times that we remember for years to come. They may occur as we drive home after attending the funeral of a grandparent, as grief is being expressed. Or when a young child decides that it is *his* turn to tell you a story, since you have told him bedtime stories for the past three years. Or when you as a parent arrive home after unexpectedly having lost your job, only to have your children embrace and comfort you. Or when you spend a day at the beach and enjoy an unusually beautiful sunset together. Or when you look at old family movies or slides together.

Quality moments can happen during difficult, crisis times—when there has been a tragedy or disappointment, just as often as they occur during the easier, less stressful times. But whenever they occur, quality moments build a "scrapbook" of family memories that will be brought out by family members through reminiscing for years to come.

But Remember the Quantity of Time

I have heard parents say, "We really don't have much *quantity* time, but we do have *quality* time together." For most families, this is not an either-or choice. Without having an adequate *quantity* of time, there is not adequate opportunity for those unexpected *quality* moments to occur.

Yet we would not be making the best use of our time if we just sit passively waiting for quality experiences. Quality moments can be facilitated by structuring our time.

For example, families can profit from getaway times— days, weekends, or longer vacation times when there is not the distraction of jobs, school, homework, and chores. Removing such distractions can make closeness a greater possibility—as long as such getaways do not become another kind of work. Relaxing and enjoying informal activities can be both enjoyable and memorable.

At other times, families find that stay-at-home days can be of value. With our life-in-the-fast-lane pace, scheduling a time for chores as well as favorite family activities can help build family togetherness.

Family times can be enjoyed by the entire family, or they may be times when one parent spends time alone with one child.

In a two-parent family, the parents will need an evening away from the children. Single parents also need time away from the children to enjoy adult relationships.

As a spouse and parent, I have found the value of structuring our family time as carefully as I can. How easy it is to live a reactive style of family life—reacting to circumstances and time demands rather than setting goals and putting energy and time into what we say we value.

A family calendar is essential for the effective use of time. In addition to writing down the obligations of each family member, special times for the entire family—away or at home—are scheduled. Even though there may be occasional emergencies and thus a need for flexibility, these calendared-in family times are seen as important by family members. All persons in a family provide input as to what will happen in these family times. Some families find value in having each family member in turn make a choice as to the activity that the family will do on these occasions.

However you structure the decision-making process, it is essential that families do what is enjoyable and relaxing, as an antidote to all of the worries, frustrations, and stresses that can plague us.

If we don't work to keep our calendars in control, they tend to start controlling us, until we are living with the "tyranny of the urgent"—a life-style that consists mainly of "putting out fires," reacting chaotically to stresses and problems. We should aim to become more assertive in making

choices and plans that enhance the family health and togetherness we all want so much.

Balance Is the Key

This proper use of time is one of the greatest difficulties
I have faced as a parent. My greatest challenge has been to
keep the proper balance between work, study, and play that
is so essential for personal and family well-being.

Sometimes I feel as if I am sitting on a teeter-totter in a
park. If I am not careful, I find myself either flying up into
the air and out of control, or crashing down to the ground
with a thud. Keeping a proper sense of balance and perspective requires careful monitoring. You may find it helpful, as I have, to regularly schedule opportunities to evaluate
your use of time. Every few months, try to make it a habit
to ask yourself: How am I doing with my use of time? In
what ways am I overcoming any tendencies to become too
task- or work-oriented? How can I adjust my time priorities
so that I strike a balance between work, study, and play?

Remember that the right use of time and energies will
help you and your family build a strong bond of togetherness
which can help avoid the dangers of being passive (not trying
at all) or chaotic (reacting to circumstances rather than controlling them as much as possible).

Your efforts to have both quality and quantity time with
your family are a long-term investment. Such efforts will
be valuable not only for the well-being of your family, but
for yourself as well, as you seek the right balance between
work, study, and play.

Next Steps

1. Reflect on your family's use of time during the past
week. You may want to refer to your calendar to see where
time was invested by each family member. Identify with a

colored pen the blocks of time you had together as a family. Would you call them *quantity* or *quality* time? For example, watching television together can be a valuable family activity, but it may be merely being together without any valuable interaction.

Evaluate your use of time. What choices need to be made to ensure that you have adequate time together as a family?

2. Divide a piece of paper into seven sections. Mark each section as a day of the week. As a family, plan a week that allows for individual activities and commitments but which also schedules family time. Be sure that every family member has an opportunity to give input regarding what these activities may be. If your family has not had much quality time together, you may meet resistance at this change in priorities. I encourage you to be both positive and firm about wanting to schedule in some time for the family—even if it is only one hour during the week.

3. Evaluate your own balance between work, study, and play. What needs to change in order for you to find a more effective balance?

6

Appreciation

Some of us tend to express our feelings quite openly, so that people know what we are feeling. Other people are less expressive and keep many of their feelings inside.

When Johnny comes home with his report card, for example, his mother may respond with words of affirmation and praise for his good grades. His father, on the other hand, may not say much, even if he feels good feelings inside.

When Suzie comes home feeling crushed because of what another child had said to her at school, one parent may give her a hug and remind her of how important she is to the family. The other parent may react with no response, or with a stoic comment like, "You'll just have to get used to bad times. Life is like that."

Despite our varying styles of relating, researchers have found that another essential ingredient for healthy family functioning is the open and loving expression of appreciation.

To show appreciation is to recognize the worth of another person or object. For example, if we see a car that we like, we may say something like, "Wow! Take a look at that car. It's a beauty!" Or when we see a beautiful sunset we may say, "Look at all those beautiful colors! How gorgeous!" The same goes for another person. When we recognize something they have done that we appreciate, we say, "Thank you. I really appreciate what you have done." Or we may show with our actions that we appreciate something or someone.

A Negative Mode

As we encounter stresses, frustrations, and disappointments in life, we may find ourselves getting into a negative mode, focusing on what we don't like or on the times when someone has not lived up to our level of expectations. For example, we may tend to yell at our children when they are fighting. But we may fail to acknowledge when our children do what we expect, or when they do get along and play well together. We may express our disappointments when other family members do not measure up to our ideals, but forget to express appreciation for the efforts they make to do what is right.

Such a negative approach to life is like living in a swamp or standing in quicksand. It can make people feel as if they are stuck and unhappy, without knowing what to do about it. Such negativity stifles the positive expressions of feelings and distorts communication efforts. When everything is negative, people feel defensive, since they are being attacked, criticized, or put down.

In seeking to grow healthy families, we need to watch for any tendencies to be overly negative, and to eliminate such styles of relating. (We are talking here about a communication style that is unrealistically negative and critical; this is different from constructive criticism, which at times may be necessary to correct an unacceptable situation.)

Approaching and Distancing Behaviors

Eliminating our negativity is a first step in strengthening our abilities to express appreciation to other family members. Such negativity tends to be a "distancing behavior"— behavior that puts emotional distance between people and causes estrangement. Whether it is undue criticism, focusing on weaknesses or failures, sarcasm, or put-downs, such negativities poison rather than nourish relationships. Nonverbal gestures such as turning away, frowns, sighs, or any evidence of not listening or caring will also tend to increase the distance between people.

When people do not feel appreciated, they may have one of two reactions. Some people tend to become resentful and act out their frustrations. They try to get attention by misbehavior at school or home, being unmotivated with schoolwork, and so on. Others respond by being anxious and uncertain. Their symptoms may be psychosomatic (headaches, stomachaches, and so on). They may show their feelings by refusing to talk or in other nonverbal ways. By being sick or afraid, a person may be trying to get needed attention. Both acting out and anxious reactions tend to put more distance in a family relationship.

In contrast to such "distancing behaviors" are "approaching behaviors"— any word or action that brings people closer together. Actions such as hugs, smiles, winks, strokes, little surprise gifts, or handshakes show a desire to be close. Even the way we acknowledge the need our children have for privacy (for example, by knocking on their bedroom doors before entering) can be an approaching, appreciating behavior.

Saying What We Feel

In *Fiddler on the Roof* a wife sings to her husband, "Do you love me?" The husband replies with a list of all that he does for his family—working, providing food, protecting the family, and so on. But the wife is persistent with her question, "Do you love me?" She needs to hear those words from her husband, who seems unable to express his love for her in words.

We can maximize our efforts to be appreciative by using words to show this appreciation. We can say things like, "I like being with you," or, "I'm glad we're a family," or, "I really appreciate the way you help with keeping the house picked up," or, "I love you." Listening attentively to a child is another way to show appreciation, because the child sees that he or she is important enough for us to take the time to listen and understand.

Such expressions need to be specific. For example, rather than saying, "Jennie, you're a good girl," one could say, "Jennie, I really appreciate the way you share with your baby brother."

Even though we may tend to be appreciative more readily in positive times, we should remember to be supportive and reassuring also in times of stress and conflict. Our children need to know that our love for them is not based on their actions, but on the fact that the family belongs together, no matter what happens.

Our expressions of appreciation, then, need to be given with no expectations that such affection will be given in return. As we learn to give with "no strings attached," we will "unhook" from the need to have the affection reciprocated every time. After all, such affection and affirmation is a gift to others. If the gift is returned, it is unexpected and appreciated rather than an obligation on the part of the other family member.

Giving What We Have

We can give only what we possess ourselves. Developing skills in expressing affection and appreciation is based on our own self-esteem. For example, if parents feel inadequate and are quite needy themselves, they will find it difficult to be affectionate with their children. Or they will expect massive doses of affection from their children. Such expectations cause frequent disappointment, even anger, for some parents.

Expecting our children to meet our needs becomes a "no-win" situation for both parents and children. Children begin to feel that they carry a heavy obligation to make their parents feel loved and realize that they will not be able to meet their parents' insatiable need for affection. Parents lose by depending on these efforts and becoming resentful when these needs are not being met.

We parents, then, need to develop a balanced perspective regarding our own needs for affection and appreciation. It is wonderful when our children reach out to give us a hug or tell us how much they love us. But to expect or demand such expressions is unhealthy, and even dangerous, for healthy family functioning.

When doing marriage or family counseling, I often use the FIRO-B, a test that measures the extent to which people express and need *inclusion* (feeling included, welcomed), *control* (decision making), and *affection* (verbal and nonverbal strokes and affirmations). Since we are all unique human beings, we vary considerably in the degree to which we express these phenomena and the degree to which we need them. For example, one person may be a loner and not feel much need to be in a group or involved in many relationships. Another person may have a great need for inclusion and frequently feel disappointed or left out.

The application of all of this to parenting is that our personalities and needs will affect the way we relate to our children. If we have a high need for affection, for example, we may feel disappointed or resentful with children who are not that expressive but are more independent or reserved.

As parents, we need to develop a growing awareness of our own needs, as well as where we are with our self-esteem. We all, parents and children, need to feel that we belong, have worth, and are competent. We need to appreciate ourselves as well as other family members.

Becoming Lovable

An essential step in enhancing our own self-esteem is to become lovable—to accept the gifts of appreciation and affirmation that other people give us.

Some of us have inaccurately thought that turning away or repelling such affirmations was a sign of humility. We may worry that such positive actions or words of love will "go to our head" so that we become conceited. But nothing could be farther from the truth. True, a person can become conceited, but only from an unrealistic, puffed-up sense of pride and selfishness. At heart a conceited person is really suffering from poor self-esteem, hidden behind an attempt to look, act, and feel better than other people.

Persons who are developing healthy self-esteem, on the other hand, become comfortable as others compliment or affirm them. Since such expressions—through words or actions—are really gifts from others to ourselves, we can accept them gratefully and appreciate them. For example, instead of responding to a child's appreciation for an enjoyable meal with, "Oh, it was just something I threw together," we might say, "Thank you, Timmy, I really appreciate that." Or, when a child says, "Mom, you sure look nice today," we can say, "Thank you, Suzie, I like to hear that." As we learn to be grateful and to accept the affirmation of others, we grow in self-esteem. It is these gifts of love that nourish our lives and bring new growth and confidence.

Being lovable is a potent example for our children as well. As they see us responding in a healthy way to love and appreciation, they, too, will learn these skills. And the love that we express to them will nourish their lives and help them build the confidence and sense of well-being that will help them cope with all of the stresses and adjustments of growing up.

Expressing love and appreciation is a skill that we can develop even if we did not experience it in our growing-up years. Learning to be direct, specific, and positive in our relationships with our children can build healthy families, as well as healthy individuals.

Next Steps

1. Write yourself a letter in which you list what you appreciate about yourself as an individual and as a parent. Be as specific as possible by giving examples whenever you can. After you have written the letter, reflect on how this process felt. Some of us find that we would be much more comfortable, and could write a longer letter about our weaknesses, failures, and disappointments. We can begin to turn around this negative approach by learning to affirm and appreciate ourselves.

2. Write a letter of appreciation for every other member of your family. Again, be as specific as possible. Give these letters to the others and enjoy them together.

3. As a family, do an activity called an Affirmation Bombardment. Begin with one family member. Ask that everyone else say what they especially appreciate about that person. Then move on to another person, and so on, until everyone has had the opportunity to be affirmed. If possible, share together on how this experience felt. How was it different from times of being critical or angry? How did these expressions of affirmation help your family feel a bond of love and togetherness?

7

Communication

Let's meet another family—mom and her three teenage children. They're presently eating breakfast.

Mother: Jenni, will you pass me the sugar? (*No response; Jenni continues to do her homework while eating.*) Jenni, pl-l-e-e-ase pass me the sugar!

Jenni: Huh? I'm busy. Get it yourself.

Bob: You slob, why don't you help your mother?

Jenni: I'm not a slob. Look at the milk you dribbled all over your shirt. You're the slob!

Bob: But you just spilled jam on your math book. You'll sure get in trouble for that, slob!

Tina: I hate this family. Nobody ever talks nice to each other.

Bob: (*in a mocking tone*): Oh, you're the perfect one. S-o-r-r-r-y! (*Tina runs out of the room crying, Bob shrugs his shoulders, Jenni keeps doing her homework, and mother sighs.*)

Maybe such explosions never happen at your house, but they do happen in many homes. Whether they are caused by a young child who throws a tantrum, a teenager who gets up from the table and slams three or four doors, or a parent who yells at his children to stop screaming—there are times when emotions get high and a family feels it is out of control.

At the root of many of these difficult moments is a lack of effective communication—clearly saying what we mean and accurately understanding what others are communicating.

In my work as a family counselor I have found that there are often two root causes for family difficulties: lack of self-esteem in the parents or children, and lack of effective communication. Either difficulty seems to underlie so many issues and misunderstandings; when both exist in the same family, there is often havoc.

The process of communication has a great influence on the way we function as families. When people do not communicate clearly or listen accurately, many rather simple issues can get ignored, exaggerated, or distorted.

For example, I have known families for whom major battles have erupted over the kind of floor wax being used, the price of vitamins, or the thickness of hamburger patties. Once such conflicts begin, they can explode into accusations, threats, slammed doors, broken dishes, or sullen silence.

Missing the Mark

Poor communication can take several forms.

• *Lack of clarity*—speaking in a mumble, with incomplete sentences, or using words that do not make much sense. For example, a person may say, "Pass the. . ." or "Mom, stop. . . ."

● *Indirectness*—saying something about somebody outside the family and expecting the other family member to understand that what is being said is really about them. For example, a parent might say, "Now, take Bobby next door. He is so cooperative and helpful. He would never leave his room in a mess."

● *Mind reading*—expecting others to know what we are trying to say or what we want. For example, "When I clear my throat, you should know that I want more water. How specific do I need to be?"

● *Distraction*—avoiding an issue by saying something that is irrelevant or inappropriate in an attempt to get the other person to forget about what was being said. A teenager says, "Dad, when can I get my allowance?" and the father responds, "Do you know where the front section of the newspaper is?"

● *Exaggerating*—taking another person's comment too personally or blowing it out of proportion. A parent might say, "Jodi, I really need you to pick up your room." A child would be exaggerating if her response was, "You don't love me. All you think about is your house being clean!"

● *Attacking or blaming*—placing all of the responsibility on the other person, trying to make him or her feel guilty or like a failure. If a child were to say, "Can I have a dollar for lunch?" an attacking response would be, "All you think about is money. Can't you realize that money doesn't grow on trees?"

● *Withdrawing*—avoiding an issue or communication by not responding at all, or by showing feelings in nonverbal ways. For example, a child may ask, "When can I have my birthday party?" A withdrawing response would be a roll of the eyes, shrugged shoulders, a sigh, or walking out of the room.

• *Joking*—making light of a situation and not taking it seriously. A husband might tell his wife, "I'd like to tear down that old fence in the back yard. It's a mess." A joking response would be, "That reminds me of the poem about how good fences make good neighbors."

These examples show various ways in which we can "miss the mark" in communicating. Any of these poor communications can cause a family to deteriorate into frequent battles or into a stony silence of mere toleration.

The severity or complexity of the issues that a family confronts may not cause serious difficulties in the family relationship, but the quality of their communication can make a significant difference.

Saying What We Mean, Meaning What We Say

There are several important principles of effective communication that I have found helpful in enhancing family relationships.

l. Be clear.

Communication is effective only if a message is clearly stated. Any fuzziness or ambiguity will cloud the process and lead to confusion or frustration. To be clear is to be specific, and to say things in such a way that there are no hidden messages or double meanings.

At times, we may not know for sure what we are truly feeling about a particular concern. In such cases, it is important to say that we are feeling unsure or unclear. And if we ask the other person to help us explore our feelings, we will have taken a significant step toward understanding ourselves and others.

2. Be congruent.

To be congruent means that what we feel inside and what we want to communicate is what we are actually saying.

Our words, our facial expressions, the movements of our bodies, and the tone of our voices need to match in order for there to be clear communication. Consequently, sarcasm or body language that communicates the opposite of what our words are communicating will only cause difficulties in the communication process.

3. Share feelings directly and nonjudgmentally.

In a family, communication will not always be positive or simple. Frustrations, disappointments, and adjustments can make family life rocky and tense, and effective communication during those times can be one of the greatest challenges we face.

Some of us have shorter fuses than others: we get angry quickly. Others seem to be able to take a great deal more before they finally explode. No matter what your style, remember that we need to communicate our feelings in ways that are not blaming or judging. Even when we are sharing frustrations, we can say, "Johnny, I feel very frustrated when you jump up from the table when we are trying to discuss this issue." This is much better than, "You inconsiderate little brat! You're acting just like your father!" When we blame or judge, other people tend to react with defensiveness or hostility. This only raises the level of tension and distorts the communication process even further.

Feeling angry or frustrated is normal. I wonder about persons who say that they never feel angry. My guess is that they really do, but that such feelings tend to get denied, repressed, or displaced.

How we express these feelings is the key point. We can share our feelings without using them as a weapon to attack others. Developing this skill can take a great deal of energy and commitment, especially if we grew up in homes where this attacking style was quite typical, or if we have hair-trigger tempers.

4. Stay as relaxed as you can.

Communication is most effective when it takes place in a relaxed atmosphere. Such open, free times help people feel less threatened, so they are willing to share what they are really feeling.

Some situations or issues may be so touchy that the tension begins to intensify as the communication continues. Voice levels may rise, faces may grow tense, and the result is an angry exchange rather than effective communication.

Certain times of the day may be better for effective communication than others. A poor time for communication is before breakfast. We are much better equipped to share and listen to each other after we have a little food in our stomachs. Issues are also not effectively handled when people are ready to walk out the door, or after they are in bed ready to go to sleep. Trying to resolve a problem at either of these times may cause further frustration or estrangement.

If you find that a particular issue arouses a great deal of anxiety or hostility, you may need to postpone the discussion until tempers are under control. But be sure that with the postponement, there is a commitment to set a time when the communication can take place. Otherwise, postponements become a way to avoid or ignore these issues.

5. Listen accurately.

Listening is an essential part of the communication process, and it may be a skill that we need to enhance.

In listening to someone, we can show our interest by

making eye contact, focusing on the other person, and using appropriate gestures (such as nods of the head or concerned looks) that show we are listening.

What many of us tend to do is to react rather than to listen. Note this process in the following conversation.

Son: Mom, can we go out for dinner tonight?
Mom: I don't want to go. I'm too tired.
Son: But we don't have anything good to eat at home. And I'm hungry for a pizza.
Mom: Is food all you can think about?
Son: No, but I'm hungry for pizza.
Mom: And who's going to pay for it? I don't get paid until Friday.
Son: You never do what I want to do! Let's forget the whole idea.

Notice in that conversation (which turned into a confrontation) that neither person really heard the other. Instead, they reacted to each other until the tension level went up and tempers flared.

A constructive alternative is for each person to focus on what the other person is saying before responding. Thus, the goal is to understand one another, rather than just to react to what had been said.

Let's try the conversation between the son and his mother again, but this time have them use more effective listening skills to see how this influences the outcome of the communication.

Son: Mom, can we go out for dinner tonight?
Mom: It sounds to me like you'd rather eat out than at home.
Son: Yeah, all we seem to have is leftovers, and we haven't had pizza for a while.

Mom: I hear you. That sounds good to me, too, but I have a concern that we need to consider.

Son: What's that?

Mom: Well, I don't get paid until Friday. And we're just about out of cash. I don't know how we would pay for the pizza.

Son: Sounds like money is the problem. I've got an idea. I got paid yesterday for my lawn jobs. How about if I take you out to dinner?

Mom: That sounds like a great idea. Let's get ready!

Notice how each person heard the other, and how effectively the issue was handled. I realize that many communications may not be that simple, but the principle is the same. If we take the time to listen and understand someone, we will not minimize the other person's feelings or exaggerate what is being discussed.

Notice that an essential part of the listening process is feeding back a response to the person to check out the accuracy of our understanding. Beginning a sentence with "Do you mean . . . ?" or "It sounds like . . . " can be effective ways to check this out. In so doing, you may realize that your interpretation of the message is not quite what was intended. Checking it out gives the other person opportunity to clarify or amplify the original message.

You may also find that the other person did not really mean what he or she said. Your response can help clarify the true message, so that the communication is kept clear and understandable.

6. *Be persistent.*

When tempers flare, we may back off or walk away, hoping that somehow things will work out, even though the communication process has not been completed. But backing off (except to postpone the discussion for a short time) is rarely helpful. Instead, anger and resentment can build until there is an even more tumultuous explosion. Or the anger may come out "sideways" through sarcasm or putdowns.

When we may feel like backing off or giving up, we need to hang in there. Staying in touch with our children and being persistent in a loving way can greatly enhance the communication process. Persistence, when it is both firm and flexible, can show our children that we do care, that we do want to understand and listen to each other.

The Scriptures tell us, "Do not let the sun go down while you are still angry" (Eph. 4:26). Before the end of every day try to resolve any tensions before bedtime. It's amazing how unresolved tensions tend to deaden feelings or intensify anger, if they are allowed to build from day to day. If we monitor our issues or tensions, they will not build into insurmountable obstacles in our relationships.

Many families discover that their relationships deteriorate due to neglect or withdrawal. They tend to strengthen through sincere and persistent efforts to deal with feelings and needs.

7. Apologize and forgive.

When we have done or said something wrong or inappropriate, we need to apologize to our children. This can be healthy not only for the well-being of our family relationships, but also for ourselves, as we realize that even as adults we can make mistakes, blow up, or do something regrettable.

With apologizing we also need to forgive. We may feel tempted to hold in resentment and not let go of alleged violations our children have committed in word or deed.

Repressing these resentments will serve only to widen the breach and deaden the feelings in our relationships. Learning to forgive—to let go, to be willing to move on, to accept the human frailties of our family members even as we accept our own—is an essential step in becoming emotionally healthy.

When a disturbance has caused problems in a family, apologizing and forgiving are effective ways of "clearing the air." Without these dynamics, our efforts may feel frustrating or fruitless. With them, we have taken significant strides towards reconciliation and understanding.

Note how these ingredients of healthy family functioning interweave with each other. Without a deepening sense of commitment, we may feel like giving up and not trying to stay in touch. And without enough quantity and quality time, there may not be adequate opportunity to develop a bond of togetherness. And without effective communication and listening skills, the process of growing and loving may be stifled or subverted. Each of these dynamics is needed if we are to become families that are enriching, fulfilling, and loving.

Next Steps

1. Reflect on the communication patterns in your family of origin—when you were a child, as well as today. Would you call your family members effective, average, or weak communicators and listeners? Have these patterns changed over the years? What changes could you initiate when you are with them now?

2. Think of an issue or concern that causes repeated friction or tension between another family member and you.

Use this structured communication exercise to deal with the issue:

Step 1. Ask the other person to share his or her feelings and opinions about the issue for 5-10 minutes. During this time, you listen attentively, but don't respond verbally.

Step 2. Take 3-5 minutes to express in your own words what you heard. When the other person says, "Yes, that's what I meant," you can move on to the next step. Otherwise, repeat Steps 1 and 2 until there is agreement on the message being sent and your understanding of it—but not necessarily agreement on the issue.

Step 3. Reverse the roles, so that you share your feelings and reflections on the concern, while the other person listens attentively.

Step 4. Then the other person expresses to you what was heard. As with Steps 1 and 2, if you agree that the other person has heard your message, move on to Step 5. Otherwise, repeat Steps 3 and 4 until there is agreement between communicator and listener.

Step 5. Evaluate how this process helped you understand one another.

8

Conflict Resolution

One of the myths we encounter is that the good life is supposed to be free of pain or conflict. That seems to be the ideal toward which many people aspire. There are thousands of drugs available to deal with pain or discomfort (and certainly such drugs can be helpful when pain is a significant problem). But for some people, even a little pain or discomfort is unacceptable. Conflict also seems to be unacceptable.

But no matter how hard we try, there is no way to avoid conflicts completely. They are a natural part of life. Family wellness cannot be measured necessarily by the number of conflicts a family faces, but rather by the manner in which these conflicts are handled.

My concern, then, is not that conflicts be totally eliminated, although if we can prevent conflicts and resolve our differences more effectively, family life can be enhanced. Instead, my concern is that we learn ways to resolve conflicts, so that the focus is not on who wins or loses, or who has the power, but on keeping the family relationship intact, and even strengthening it.

Ineffective Conflict Resolution

A number of approaches to resolving conflicts are ineffective and even harmful.

● *Intimidation*—using an excessive amount of power in order to resolve conflicts. For example, a parent may say, "I don't care how you feel. I'm your parent. Do it! On occasion that may be necessary, but it does not lay a solid basis for effective conflict resolution. Such an intimidating, overbearing style often leads to feelings of powerlessness and resentment on the part of the child and can lead either to passive withdrawal or more rebellious behavior.

● *Abdication*—the opposite extreme from an intimidating style, abdication is letting the child make the decisions, as a way to avoid tension or conflicts. A parent may say, "I don't care. You decide. You always get your way anyhow!"

Abdicating often comes from a person who feels both powerless and resentful. It may be a form of manipulation to get the child to act in a certain way.

Whatever its motive, abdication is not healthy for either the child or the parent. Some structure of authority is essential for the family to function in a healthy manner.

● *Avoidance*—denying that there is an issue, or attempting to sweep it under the rug. Some people hope that conflicts will just go away if they are ignored. Unfortunately, most conflicts just remain temporarily in the shadows, only to return later in a more potent or complex way.

Avoiding conflicts also creates an unreal environment in the family. The appearance is that all is well, but when one scratches the surface of family functioning, there may be deep and unresolved problems.

● *Distortion*—either minimizing or exaggerating the conflict. Some people will minimize a conflict by saying, "That's not a real problem. Look at what some families have to deal with!" Or they may say, "No big deal. Let's not worry about it. Everything will work out all right."

Other people can make a relatively minor problem into a major battle. For them any question or difference of opinion is a challenge to parental authority, loyalty, love, or commitment. Such a parent might say, for example, "If you really love me, you'll stop disagreeing with me!"

One of the greatest challenges in resolving a conflict is to agree on its size—not seeing it smaller or larger than it really is. Unless there is agreement on this issue, a family may get more frustrated or angry as attempts are made to resolve the conflict.

• *Getting stuck*—trying to resolve a problem but being unsuccessful. Persons may passively shrug their shoulders and say, "I don't know what to do. We tried that once." Or the response may be a more stubborn refusal to budge— or even to talk.

A family may feel stuck if an issue continues to grow in intensity over a period of days, weeks, or months. Or this stuck feeling may occur when the same problem keeps coming up again and again.

Either way, a family may find that their life together seems to revolve more and more around the same issue— whether it's the choice of clothing, household chores, proposed activities, or curfews.

• *Gunnysacking*—holding in resentful feelings from the past. When people have not learned to forgive and let go of past hurts or disappointments, they tend to bury these feelings inside, where they fester and grow, causing more hurt and bitterness. Then a person may bring out all of these old hurts and dump them on the other person. Bringing up old hurts serves only to cloud the current issue, delay its effective resolution, and cause more misunderstanding and estrangement.

• *Sabotage*—saying something or acting in a way that destroys the process of resolving conflicts. This can be done indirectly through many of the ineffective methods described above, such as gunnysacking, getting stuck, distorting, or avoiding. The sabotaging can be done by either the child or the parent. But no matter who stifles the process, it results in an unhealthy situation in which nobody wins—not even the person who thinks a battle is won by postponing the discussion. When conflicts keep festering away like a disease, there are no winners. The conflicts only cause more problems later.

Who's Got the Power?

One of the most touchy but significant concerns related to resolving conflicts is that of power. In some families the parents have all the power, which we call an *authoritarian* approach. In other families, the children have the power, which we call a *permissive* approach.

In between these two extremes is an approach that seems to work quite well for most conflicts—an approach that is more *democratic* in style. To be democratic is first to realize that parents are indeed leaders in their families. They do not need to abdicate all power, but conflicts will be more effectively resolved if this power is shared with the children. In this way, every member of the family will feel a greater commitment to the proposed resolution.

This sharing of power will vary with the age of the children. With very young children we probably will not share parental power on many decisions. But as children learn to talk and to make their own decisions, we need to be sure that they are making some decisions on their own and that we include them in family discussions whenever it seems appropriate.

As children become teenagers, they need to feel included in the process more and more. Soon they will be adults themselves—at least in a physical sense. And if we are to help prepare them for the challenges and responsibilities of adulthood, we need to give them increasing freedom, as well as a voice in setting rules and resolving conflicts.

How can this sharing of power be handled? It may begin during the preschool years with having the children choose the clothes they will wear from among those in their closets. The process continues on until the children are choosing their hobbies, sports, and other activities. Then during the teenage years, we may want to give our children a clothing allowance, so they can select their own clothes.

The specifics will vary from family to family and child to child, but the goals need to be the same: to be sure that children have an increasing amount of independence and freedom, an amount that seems appropriate and helpful in facilitating the movement toward independence and maturity.

This need for increasing independence is an issue which will have to be discussed regularly throughout the years our children are still living at home. With understanding and the willingness to listen, this process can be marked by enthusiasm and confidence, rather than by conflict and disharmony.

An Effective Process

For effective conflict resolution to take place in families, adequate time needs to be set aside for families to deal with conflicts and concerns. And as the conflicts are being considered, the use of effective communication and listening skills will greatly help the process. Reassurances and expressions of appreciation, as well as reminders of the commitment people have to each other, will also encourage the persons to keep the conflicts in perspective. The atmosphere should be one of, "We know that we love and care about each other. We're a family. Let's try to work this out together."

There are several essential steps in effective conflict resolution.

1. Identify the issue.

Identifying the issue may seem like a relatively simple task, but many families find it difficult. The key issue for one person may be quite different for another. For example, a family may be having a conflict over the time a teenager should be home at night. The teenager may be mainly concerned about the time the parents are setting. The parents, on the other hand, may be more concerned about the activity the teenager is attending (a more mature movie, a rock concert, or a party at someone else's home), or by the fact that the teenager will be driving to this event.

As these family members seek to identify the specific problem, they can explore their feelings and concerns so that the conflict can be pinpointed. This process of identifying the issue does not usually work well at the door as the teenager is leaving. Such plans should have been discussed together earlier in the day, so that adequate time is available for the discussion.

Sometimes more than one issue is involved. Disentangling these issues and dealing with them one at a time can be a helpful way to simplify the process, as well as to sharpen the needed negotiation skills.

2. Brainstorm alternatives.

Often there may be more than one alternative to resolving a conflict. A time for brainstorming these alternatives—when family members feel free to think of options without evaluating them—can greatly facilitate the process.

Some families actually list their thoughts on paper—either as a group, or individually—followed by sharing in the group. Either way, family members will be encouraged to use their creativity to find solutions that are acceptable to everyone else whenever possible.

The process of brainstorming encourages families to use their heads, rather than just their feelings, in resolving conflicts. If we base family interaction only on feelings, there tend to be many more heated arguments. And the conflicts may mushroom into problems that are bigger and more complex than are necessary.

We can simplify the process by dealing with conflicts in a way that energizes our creative process and sets aside our ego involvement as much as possible. For example, a family dealing with a concern about a teenager driving a long distance to a concert may think of the following options.

● The teenager can drive, but will need to be home at an hour that is acceptable to the parents.

● The parents will drive the teenager and friends.

● The driving will be shared by the parents and the parents of another teenager.

● If public transportation is available, the group will travel that way.

● The teenagers will choose another activity that concludes at an earlier hour and is held in a safer part of town.

Each family can think of their own creative alternatives for every conflict that they face. Thinking of these options is an essential part of coming to acceptable resolutions.

3. Choose an acceptable option.

Once a list of at least a few alternatives has been identified, family members can work to evaluate the options and choose one which seems acceptable to everyone.

We have found it helpful to begin by first eliminating options that everyone agrees will probably not work. Usually, at least one or two ideas can be eliminated quite easily.

Once you have narrowed the list down to two or three options, the discussion may become more intense. Work together to think through each of these options carefully, listing positives and negatives for each option.

Then select the one that the family thinks will work best. The more a family makes consensus its goal, the more realistic a goal it becomes. Yet consensus may not always be possible. Then the family might agree that first the teenager's option will be tried, but that next time, the parents' alternative will be followed.

Consensus may not always be a realistic goal. On some issues that involve safety or important values, the parents may need to say no or limit the options under consideration. As we work toward a more democratic process, we do not abdicate the authority we have as parents. We may have to take a stand on certain issues, but it is best if there are not too many of these. When they do arise, we still need to discuss them thoroughly, so that we can explain why we feel so strongly. In this way the children see that we are trying to be thoughtful and considerate, rather than just arbitrary.

With frequent reassurances of love and commitment, conflicts can often be resolved. The goal is not who wins, but how the family feels about itself and about the process after the conflict has been resolved.

4. Evaluate what happened.

Once an option has been selected, family members need to commit themselves to implementing it with every bit of energy and effort that will be needed.

After a period of time—as long as is necessary for people

to see how the option has worked—the family needs to sit down once again and evaluate what happened. Questions such as the following can be helpful:

• How did this option work? Did it work out the way that people thought it would? If not, what did happen?

• In what ways was this alternative not as successful or acceptable as it might have been? In what ways was it successful or acceptable?

• Should the family try the first option again, or is it time to move on to another alternative?

• Which of the other options does the family agree to try next? Why is this alternative the best of the ones that were listed?

Again, this process may take a great deal of time and effort. Both parents and children may need to muster all of their creativity and objectivity in dealing with these concerns. But the results will be of great value for family health and happiness. Rather than denying or distorting issues, the family is learning to deal with them in an open manner, so that the family bond becomes strengthened, even as the thoughts, opinions, and needs of each family member are validated and explored.

Moving On

Having conflicts in our families is not a sign of weakness or dysfunction. Conflicts are a part of everyday life. And conflicts are not necessarily a sign of a lack of loyalty or commitment. Instead, they are often based on a difference of opinion, different values, or varying needs. Conflicts are also complicated by such factors as hunger, fatigue, moods, and the overall environment in the home at any particular time.

Once a conflict has been dealt with, no matter how heated or difficult the process may have been, families need to move on, to let go of any anger or frustration they felt over the conflict or the process used to resolve it.

Some people tend to hang on to their feelings, so that they may not truly give the agreed upon alternative a chance. Others may resent the fact that there was disagreement at all, as if a sign of our children's loyalty is their complete agreement on every issue and concern. But if a family sees conflicts as an opportunity to stretch and strengthen their skills of relating together, conflicts can become an expected part of everyday family life.

Then no matter how intense the conflicts may be, we can learn to let go of our feelings and move on with life. The family relationship needs to be seen as larger and more important than any specific issue.

Sometimes we may need to forgive the others—if we feel that our feelings have been hurt or if we feel rejected or neglected. But learning how to let go of these feelings, and not nurse them like wounds, will help us overcome any tendency to get bitter or distant. And, in the process, our abilities to approach and deal with family concerns will get more effective and more fulfilling for everyone.

Next Steps

1. Reminisce on how conflicts were handled in your family of origin. Were they handled effectively or ineffectively? Who had the power in your family? How do you think that style has affected the way you resolve conflicts today with your own family?

2. Reflect on times when specific family conflicts have been resolved, and when they have been handled unsuccessfully. What were these issues, and what made the difference in the outcome?

3. Think of a current issue or conflict your family is experiencing. Work together to use the suggested process for dealing with this issue. Monitor what happens in the process. What seems to be the most difficult step for family members? Don't worry if the process is not completely successful the first time. Keep working at it. You will find that everyone can benefit from sharpening their skills in handling conflicts—children and adults alike.

9

Faith

There is perhaps no more challenging aspect of healthy family functioning than that of faith. In fact, what follows may be the most controversial chapter in the book. Even if you do not agree with what I say, I hope these comments will be helpful in guiding you to think about how faith and values relate to family life. (I have dealt with the question of values in greater depth in the book *Rights, Wrongs, and In-Betweens.*)

Studies of healthy families have found that some kind of common religious or moral belief system is a part of being a healthy family. In a world in which we are so bombarded with varying value systems and religions, our faith can be more essential than ever. As I share my thoughts in this chapter, I want you to know that my own faith has centered in the historic beliefs of the Christian faith as found in the teachings of the Scriptures.

My concern here is to see how faith can influence families so as to help them become strong and healthy.

How Firm a Foundation

As we begin this discussion, let's look first at some preliminary or foundational concerns.

Since the beginning of recorded history, people have had an inner drive to find meaning or make sense out of life. They have been motivated to deal with such questions as:

- What do I want to do with my life? In what ways can I best use my gifts and talents?
- How can I make life meaningful and fulfilling?
- What are my values?
- Is there a God who brings meaning to life?
- How do I account for the hatred, violence, and unhappiness that I see all around me?
- Is there life after death? And, for that matter, is there life after birth?
- What religious system or set of beliefs seems to best account for life as I experience it, with all its perplexities and ambiguities?

It is our faith or beliefs that help us come to terms with questions like these.

The Value of Faith

To believe in a certain religion is not necessarily to get wrapped up in something unrelated to life. True, some religions seem to be more "other-worldly" than relevant to life as we experience it, but one of the qualities of a vibrant faith is that it is very relevant to living. There are a number of reasons why faith is essential.

1. Faith provides a framework for dealing with the perplexities of life.

There certainly are rights and wrongs in life, but, increasingly there seem to be many "in-betweens" that can make us feel confused or upset. Faith can give us under-standing and direction for confronting these difficulties.

2. Faith can give a sense of inner peace.

In encountering conflicts in our families and elsewhere, we may find ourselves exhausted or burned out from trying to resolve these difficulties. Our faith can give us a feeling of peace, a sense of relief. Faith brings comfort.

3. Faith can give us power to face our difficulties.

A vibrant faith can give people courage to deal with what may at times seem overwhelming. It brings power to grapple with life. We know that we are not alone. We believe that there is a God who hears, understands, and is with us in whatever happens.

4. Faith can motivate us to develop relationships with other people.

Although this book is about family relationships, there is value in having friendships outside the family as well. To expect our families to meet all of our emotional and relational needs is to place an enormous—and unrealistic—burden on them.

Committing ourselves to a growing faith will bring us into contact with persons who share similar beliefs and values. This may happen through a structured organization such as a church, or a more unstructured group of friends we de-velop on our own.

Such relationships can be helpful in creating a support network—persons with whom we can share, those who will encourage and support us in times of personal and family difficulties.

As for Me

Even as a child, I felt what someone has described as a "God-shaped vacuum" in my heart—an inner desire or need for a relationship with God. I did not know exactly what that meant at the time, but I realized that I wanted to believe in a God who loved and cared for me.

For me there has been an important distinction between *faith* (belief in God) and *religion* (the practice or activities of faith). My faith in God has continued to grow and develop over the years. There have been many times when God was very real to me at a personal level. These experiences have given me a sense of peace and balance which has helped me deal with the disappointments, stresses, and heartbreaks I have encountered in life. Even in the midst of great difficulty, my life has not fallen apart very often. And when circumstances seemed "out of control," my faith helped me gain a larger perspective on life, to see beyond my immediate difficulties to what I could learn and how I could grow through these hard times.

My faith has been tested a number of times, and I have wondered more than once if there was a better belief system than the one that I had accepted. But even those times of doubt have strengthened my life as I have confirmed and clarified my beliefs.

In contrast to my experience with *faith*, my experience with *religion* has been more ambivalent. Having been brought up in a church and very active in it, I began my adult pilgrimage with a strong commitment to church involvement. In fact, my earliest career was working full time in a church setting.

Since then my experience in churches has varied. Some churches have been meaningful and helpful; others have been stressful and unhelpful. I am still not entirely sure what has made the difference for me.

I have found that when I am in a setting where people are real, in the sense of being honest about their own struggles and needs, I am comfortable to be myself and to relate my faith meaningfully to my life.

In some churches I have found confusion between *faith* and *religion*. For some people church attendance or involvement is the only indication of faith. Their religion consists of religious formalities with little concern as to how their religion relates to their family relationships or other aspects of living.

For some people overinvolvement in religion can have the same counterproductive results as can overinvolvement in any other area of life. A person can become burned out or resentful because of the constant outflow of energy into church-related activities. Or people can get totally wrapped up in a single issue (like abortion or the end of the world) and focus all their energies on that issue, as if it were all there is to religion or faith.

One of my greatest challenges has been to find the right balance between the inner and outer dimensions of my faith—the inner reflection and growth, and the outer practices of it. The pendulum so easily swings from one extreme to the other.

To find a good balance means that I meditate, pray, study, and worship as a means of deepening my personal faith. I also practice my faith in my relationships with other people and in making decisions.

My belief in God is at the core of who I am and what I am becoming. I am increasingly at peace with this dimension of my life, even though I continue to struggle with the religious outworkings of this faith.

Faith and Family

What is crucial to me, as well as to many other religious people, is that faith be relevant to everyday living, such as in family relationships. My faith needs to be meaningful to me not only in a personal way, but also in a relational sense.

One measure of our faith is how it affects these relationships. Does our faith bring clarity, love, and a healthy attitude to our families? If it does, then our faith is meaningful. If not, then we need to reflect on what has caused our faith to become sterile, ingrown, or ineffective.

The Christian faith maintains the need for a balance between faith and works. A person of faith demonstrates that faith through attitudes, behaviors, and words, in relation with family members and other people. Some people can talk about faith in such a way that one thinks they have their lives in order. But "the proof of the pudding" comes in how they relate in intimate relationships, not only in what they say they believe.

Perhaps one of the reasons why research does not seem to indicate any one religion contributing more than another to healthy family life is that most religions share a common core: a belief in the dignity of people (being made in God's image); a belief in God as a source of love, power, and insight; the need for a support system of others with whom we can share and grow; and the need to reflect beliefs in our everyday lives (the primacy of love).

We may continue to disagree on points of theology, and I would not want to stop these dialogs and discussions. But the key point in thinking about healthy families is that one of the primary "thermometers" of our faith is the quality of our relationships with other people, such as other family members, not the amount of activity in a religious organization such as a church. I do not mean that when we have "down" times in our families that this necessarily means that the dynamic of our faith is the chief culprit. But we do need to consider how our faith and beliefs can influence our family relationships.

When faith and family are brought together, we have the potential for both personal and interpersonal happiness, because then we are dealing with the meaning and purpose of life, our values, and how all of this relates to the most foundational area of our lives—our families.

Because our family experience continues to grow and change, we need to possess a vibrant faith that also continues to grow and deepen. Rather than seeking to reinforce what we already believe or have already experienced, we will want to question, examine, search, and learn, as well as enjoy. We will need the framework of a belief system, and the encouragement and support which belonging to a group of people with similar beliefs can bring.

Building on the Positive

One of the difficulties in some families occurs when there is not a general agreement regarding religion or faith. Lack of harmony in this area has caused many conflicts in families, but this need not be true. A family can exist satisfactorily when there is substantial disagreement, if they have come to terms with this concern in a way that is acceptable to the family members.

For example, I have known a family in which the two parents are from two different racial groups, as well as two different religions. One might think that such situations would be destined for failure, and I am sure that many may be. But this couple has invested a great deal of time and energy in exploring what they do have in common, and they accept their differences. Consequently, they frequently attend worship services in each other's religion. And they have involved their child in both religions, while giving the child the freedom to make his own choice some day.

This family has done what all of us probably need to do—explore our religious beliefs in the same way that we discuss any other family concern. Areas of agreement in belief and practices can be identified, as can areas where there are distinct differences. If possible, those differences can be accepted—and even appreciated. Such deliberations and decisions take a great deal of maturity and flexibility, because religion is one of those areas that can be quite touchy, causing defensiveness or outbreaks of conflict.

To acknowledge the importance of our faith is also to realize that achieving conformity in our faith may be quite difficult. Perhaps total agreement should not be our goal. As in other areas of life, we need to be more accepting and understanding of the opinions and beliefs of other people. Such an attitude of toleration can greatly enhance the emotional environment in our homes and will encourage our children to explore paths of faith for themselves throughout their lives.

I hope that these reflections have stirred some thoughts and feelings as you reflect on your own faith and how it can relate to your family relationships. Just as our families can grow in spending quality time together, communicating with each other, and showing love and appreciation, families can benefit from a growing faith that is the foundation of all that is and is yet to come.

Next Steps

1. Reflect on your own faith and values. How are they different from when you were a child? How has your faith

grown and developed? In what ways are you like and different from your parents in this regard? How has your faith affected your family relationships?

2. Identify areas of agreement and disagreement in your family concerning faith. In what ways can you build on the areas of agreement? What may need to be done regarding areas of disagreement or disharmony? How can an acceptance of differences lead to greater family harmony?

3. If you are a person with no acknowledged system of beliefs, clarify the values that do guide your everyday living. Are there any changes you would like to make at this time? What are they?

PART THREE

WHEN A FAMILY NEEDS HELP

10

When Nothing Seems to Work

Perhaps as we have considered the various ingredients of family wellness, you are feeling quite positive about your family's health. You know that there are always areas that need more attention, but generally you feel quite confident about the direction in which your family is going.

But perhaps you responded with discouragement or despair. You are caught in the midst of difficult circumstances and the differences or conflicts that exist among family members seem unresolvable. You may feel that you have tried just about everything, and nothing seems to work.

If you are discouraged, this chapter has been written especially for you.

Acknowledging the Situation

One of the key steps for overcoming difficult circumstances is to acknowledge that such a situation exists.

Many people and families invest a great deal of energy in denying their difficulties. On the outside they seem happy and fully functioning. Others may even see them as model families. But on the inside—at home, behind closed doors— the story may be quite different. There may be a quiet estrangement—a mutual toleration marked by silence or resentment. Or there may be open conflict, with a constant barrage of attacks, verbal or physical. It is unfortunate that some families invest so much energy in pretending that all is well, when it is not.

Honesty regarding what is happening is essential to growth, as painful as such acknowledgments may be. I admit that being honest can be quite difficult. Sometimes it may seem expedient to deny what is really happening, and not every family member may be as ready to face reality either. But taking this high-risk step can begin a process that can result in change, growth, and greater happiness and health. But to stay stuck in the quagmire of your current situation is to relegate yourselves to a life-style that is both unfulfilling and unnecessary.

Accepting Differences

Another essential step in getting unstuck is accepting some of the differences that exist among family members. As with acknowledging the situation, accepting differences may also be painful and feel risky.

Some families assume that conformity among family members in values, tastes, temperaments, dress styles, and goals is important. Such families tend to put great pressure on each other to conform to whatever the standard is, whether it has been determined by the family itself, the culture, or a religious group.

But learning to accept and appreciate our differences is a key part of being a healthy family. And just how to do this may seem quite puzzling.

Think for a few minutes about each of your family members. Identify ways in which they are different from one another. Do you find that these differences are irritating, or that they enhance your family life? For example, one child may be especially neat and like to keep the house in order. Another may be more neglectful, but may show more affection. One child may be more expressive of feelings, while another is more withdrawn. Every person is unique in countless ways. These differences can bring a spirit of togetherness to our families, if we can learn to appreciate these diversities.

If our goal is conformity (what I call "cookie-cutter families"—in which every family member is expected to be just like all the others), our lives will become bland or boring. Differences are not tolerated, and there may often be a power struggle to get everyone to conform.

I know it can be quite gratifying when our children adopt our values and goals, but in order for those values and goals to belong at a deeply personal level to our children, the children may need to go through a time of questioning or challenging them. Children who merely adopt their family's values and beliefs without question often challenge them even more vehemently later in life.

Especially during their teenage years, our children are exposed to conflicting value systems, through contemporary music, friends, adults, school, or church. Part of growing up is learning to evaluate these systems and develop one that is meaningful and personally acceptable.

During this process, parents may feel most threatened, for many of the values they hold dear may be drawn into question. During such encounters a family should try to use its best communication and listening skills.

Such questioning does not necessarily mean that there is no loyalty to the family. As teenagers wrestle with a number of moral and emotional issues, they often find themselves caught in both uncertainty and conflict. If at all possible, parents will strengthen their families by reassuring their children of their love and commitment.

What complicates this whole matter is that some parents have a great need for acceptance by their children. When family values or morals get drawn into question, parents may feel either slighted or rejected.

Remember that our goal as parents is to work ourselves out of a job, so to speak. We want our children to become independent adults who can think and act for themselves. We really do not want children who have to live at home for the rest of their lives, or who have to call home when faced by even the smallest kind of decision. We want children who are mature in every sense of the word.

A risky part of this task is realizing that our children may not necessarily have the same values or perspectives that we have. Some children may become more liberal than their parents regarding values and politics. Others may be more conservative.

One of the very tangible areas of difference may be varying opinions regarding clothing. Even with very young children, there may be conflict over what clothes will be worn to preschool. And these differences can accelerate into heated arguments by the time the children are adolescents. The choice of clothing is symbolic of the many choices that have to be made in life. Increasingly, children will dress in ways that please themselves and their peers rather than their parents.

In some families the issue of clothing is dealt with by having a few choices available in the child's closet. In this way, the child has a choice, and the parent does not have to get up early every morning to wash the same dress or pants worn the previous day! We find that making such choices the night before can prevent conflicts, since there is usually less anxiety than in the morning.

Despite these helps, there may still be moments of disagreement. I know parents who usually allow their children to choose their own clothing. When the choice is something the parents are uncomfortable with or embarrassed about, they pin a note of disclaimer to the child: "This outfit was selected by the child. I had nothing to do with it!"

Some issues are much more complicated and may take commitment, faith, appreciation, time, as well as communication and conflict-resolution skills. But in these volatile times, we need to remember what family life is all about, and what our goal should be. A healthy family is like a tossed salad. Just as a good salad consists of a variety of parts (some of which may seem strange but which actually taste good together), so a family may consist of persons who are quite different in the way that they communicate, deal with their feelings, and evidence their values. But taken together, especially in a spirit of genuine acceptance, family life can be enhanced, because there is an adequate balance between family togetherness and the independence of each family member.

Setting Limits

In accepting differences we do not go beyond good sense, health, and safety. In most families, children will have reasonable guidelines for bedtime, diet, and the choice of entertainment. Most families I know do not allow their teenage children to stay out all night or skip school whenever they want. I have found that giving up all standards or structure in a family does not produce happier or healthier children.

Maintaining a consistent framework of rules and guidelines for the family is essential, but from time to time it may also need to be evaluated, with new rules instituted. What is appropriate when children are four is different from when they are 16. Also some children seem to fit readily within a family's rules, while others may push us to the limits.

Finding the intricate balance between the acceptance of differences and the setting of limits may be one of the greatest tasks facing any family. It takes the wisdom of Solomon, the faith of a saint, and the perseverance of a professional race driver!

Adjusting Our Expectations

Another dynamic that can cause difficulties is our expectations. Many times we may expect more than is possible, although occasionally it may be the opposite, so that we do not encourage our children to do as well as they can.

In learning to focus on the positive and constructive, we need to look carefully at our expectations for our children. How do we respond when they bring home their report cards? What do we expect from them regarding home chores, choice of friends, or relationships with their brothers or sisters?

None of us is perfect, and we need to be careful that we do not project our own inadequacies onto our children and expect more from them than we do from ourselves. For example, a parent who was never a good athlete may expect a child to be the star of the baseball team. Or a parent who never got very good grades at school might demand grades that are beyond the capabilities of a child. Or a parent who was a rebellious teenager might demand a degree of conformity and submissiveness that the parent could never have accepted.

One of the challenges I face as a parent is to find the proper balance between not giving enough encouragement, and putting too much pressure on. The former may cause distance or estrangement between my child and myself, while the latter may cause resentment and conflict. Again, our concern should be to help create a climate which is conducive to healthy growth and relationships. Our relationships as families should be more important than any performance in academics or sports. This loyalty and commitment should be the foundation for every one of our concerns in our families.

We may find that we have been putting too much pressure on our children, so that our efforts have been counterproductive and there is more rather than less tension. If we let go of these pressures and expectations, the situation may improve. As children and parents relax with each other, the children may put forth greater efforts. As they realize that they are on their own in sports or grades, they will learn not to depend on their parents for everything in order to be successful.

A Word of Hope

Parenting can bring occasional—or frequent—feelings of despair. We may wonder if all of this effort—both the joys and the disappointments—has been worth it. We may feel that our efforts have been for naught, that our children do not even want to be part of our families to the extent that we would want.

Remember these words: "Train a child in the way he should go, and when he is old he will not turn from it" (Prov. 22:6). Notice the qualifying phrase in this promise: "when he is old." Our children may disagree with us in both minor and major ways when they try to find their own identity and place in life. They may try several different value systems before they feel settled as adults. But our hope is that our investments in time, energy, love, and financial resources will eventually pay off. Our children may need to leave home and be on their own for a while to more fully appreciate what their families have given them.

Think back to your own experience. You may have been more than ready to leave home. But once gone, you may have begun to acknowledge the heritage and love that was there in your family, despite the disagreements or tensions.

Family togetherness, then, may be a lifetime in coming. For some people the investments in time and love do pay off right along, and their families remain strong and happy through all of their transitions and changes. But for many others the growth in family relationships will continue even after the children leave home. Some may not truly appreciate and love their parents and family until they have their own children. Then the cycle will have begun all over again.

Next Steps

1. Reflect on how differences and expectations were handled in your family of origin. Were differences readily accepted, or was there subtle or overt pressure to conform? What kind of expectations were there for you as a child and teenager? Were these expectations a source of encouragement and motivation, or did they cause tension because of being unrealistically high or low?

2. Evaluate how differences and expectations may be sources of conflict currently in your family. In what ways could changes in the acceptance of differences or the readjusting of expectations enhance your family relationships?

3. Complete the following "bridge-building" activity with another member of your family.

On the line connecting your names, write down things that you have in common (tastes in food, music, values, activities, and so on). Jot down as many as you can think of. As you identify any differences, write those down below

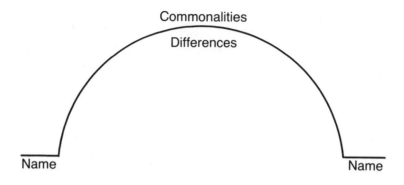

the line. In this way, the differences become the foundation of understanding, alongside the appreciation and enjoyment of what people have in common.

When you have completed the exercise, talk about whether you have more similarities or differences. What does this mean for your relationship?

Do the exercise again, this time adding in a third person, if your family has more than two persons. Again, put similarities above the "bridge," and place differences below the line. Talk about what the three of you have in common, as well as ways that you are different.

Repeat the process again, with four people, or until all members of your family have been involved. Notice that as you add more people into the activity, that there may be fewer similarities and more differences. Talk about what this means in the functioning of your family. How do family members feel about having a number of differences? How can an acceptance of these differences strengthen the family?

11

When You Don't Know What to Do Next

One of my favorite posters shows a picture of a kitten hanging by its paws from a tree limb. The expression on the cat's face indicates that it is barely hanging on. The caption is, "Hang in there, baby."

Sometimes in our families, we may feel that we are barely hanging on. It may seem that if anything else happens, we will either fall apart or run away. Most of us feel that way from time to time, and for those times, I'd like to offer a few suggestions.

The Need for Counseling

Most families have times when an outside, more objective, person can help a couple or family work through its difficulties. This may occur during a time of major change, such as after the birth of a child, when a child is an adolescent, or when one of the parents is experiencing a midlife transition.

Some people think that if a family needs counseling, it is a sign of failure or major dysfunction. This is a misunderstanding I would like to try to correct. The great majority of families I work with are within the "normal" range of behavior and experience. They have often been able to function quite well and are usually happy. But there may have been a precipitating event (such as a child's behavioral or academic problem at school) that creates a concern or crisis. During that time, a family's ability to cope may be stretched to the limit. The stress level may get so high that a family feels that everything is starting to fall apart. Or a family may recognize the warning signal of a growing sense of alienation. The conflicts may not be open but more subtle. There may be a feeling of distrust, boredom, or a lack of caring.

Whatever the problem, a family need not feel that it has failed, or that it is "mentally ill" because it desires to get some counseling. Instead, it is a sign of health that a family desires to work on what it finds troubling, so that it can move on to greater health and happiness.

If you would like to find a counselor, here are a few guidelines.

1. Look for a competent counselor.

As with any profession, there is a great variety of counselors, and thus a difference in styles, training, and competencies. The counseling profession includes the following:

● *Psychiatrists*—M.D.'s who have received special training in psychological problems. They usually work with people who are more severely mentally ill and are the only professionals who can prescribe medications for problems such as depression or nervousness.

● *Psychologists*—usually have Ph.D. degrees in psychology and are accredited by the American Psychological Association, as well as through state licensing procedures.

They usually focus on personal problems but may also specialize in marriage and family concerns.

• *Marriage and family counselors*—usually have either M.A. or Ph.D. degrees. States vary on licensing of this profession, although there is a national association with a clinical membership called the American Association of Marriage and Family Therapists. Their primary specialty, as their title indicates, is working with couples, families, and children.

• *Social workers*—usually have a master's degree in Social Work and may have special training in marriage and family relationships.

• *Pastoral counselors*—clergy who have special training in counseling. The American Association of Pastoral Counselors lists such people.

In deciding whom you should see, be sure to interview the counselor first. You have a right to find out their style of counseling, the arrangements for fees and payments, and so on. It is essential to find a counselor with whom you feel comfortable and would like to work, because the counseling process is hard work.

2. Enter counseling with an open mind.

Most people are apprehensive about counseling. They may feel uncomfortable or threatened in talking about their difficulties with a person whom they barely know.

Your attitude will make a huge difference. If you enter counseling with the expectation to grow, growth probably will happen. If, on the other hand, you are resistant to change and really do not want to be there, little will happen.

3. Growth will not occur in a continuous upward swing.

Growth in our family relationships through the counseling process rarely happens in easy, quiet ways, but rather in spurts, starts, backward steps—hopefully in an overall forward movement.

It is similar to learning how to walk. Most young children do not stand up one day and start walking and running with ease. They may begin by standing up while holding on to something or someone. Then there is the first step, often followed by a tumble, and sometimes a few moments of crying and frustration. Children usually try it again until they are able to take a few steps, then many steps—followed by running, jumping, and other more difficult movements.

Growth in our families is like that. Sometimes it takes several weeks to identify the real problems or concerns. Or there may be an uncomfortable or shocking revelation that seems to set people back. Some people feel more depressed after counseling sessions, because of the probing and exploring that takes place.

The goal of counseling is growth and change. If you find that the counseling seems to be going nowhere, then perhaps something is not working well. Maybe you need a different counselor. Or perhaps one or more family members are resisting the process and making it impossible to bring about the desired change.

It is important, though, to be patient, and give the process a chance. Many of our problems develop over a number of years, and habits or patterns may take a period of time to change.

The Value of Education

One of the difficulties regarding family relationships in our society is that we have generally used a "medical model" regarding getting help. Just as we visit a physician when we feel sick or break a leg, so we visit a psychologist or family therapist when our families are hurting.

Counseling is important. We have found the process invaluable more than once in our own family. But we can also enhance the quality of our relationships by acquiring the basic skills needed to cope in families through learning experiences.

For example, there are great numbers of books available for couples and parents (see For Further Reading). Many of these have practical guidelines for strengthening our families.

Your community may also have a variety of learning experiences available, such as the following:

• *Marriage enrichment*—a weekly series or weekend retreat focusing on marriage;

• *Parent education*—a workshop series devoted to parenting concerns;

• *Family enrichment*—a workshop or series for the entire family—parents and children together—to promote health and togetherness.

These enrichment experiences may be offered by churches or other religious organizations, community organizations such as the YMCA, schools, or others.

In addition to the value of reading and personal reflection, there are also benefits in learning in a group setting with our spouses or families. Such mutual support can help us realize that our families actually may be quite normal, after all, or at least that there are others who understand what we are experiencing.

When Separation Seems to Be the Only Answer

In extreme situations some families find that separation—marital or family—may be the only answer in order for people to survive. I do not believe that God wants us to stay in marriages or families in which there is continuing abuse or neglect, or where people are so estranged from one another that they are living only in awkward silence.

Exactly when the time for separation comes is difficult to say. Each family has its own history and experience with which to deal. But I do find that at times separation seems to be the only solution. When families have tried counseling, and when unhealthy patterns persist, something more drastic may have to be considered.

I have found that marital separation does not necessarily have to mean divorce. A time of giving "space" to each other may actually help bring a couple back together in a renewed attempt to bring about reconciliation. But, for most couples, the longer the separation, the more likely it is that the couple will stay separated.

Separation of parents and children may also be necessary. The needs or problems of some children require a special school or some other institution to give them the help they need. Some teenagers may need to live for a time in a setting other than their homes, if the situation has become critical.

When a person has graduated from high school and is still living at home, there can be great tension between parents and children. At some point parents may need to encourage or insist that their children learn to live on their own. It is best if this can be done when they are financially independent, but helping them get started with temporary financial support may be necessary.

Some families find that their relationships are enhanced when they have some distance from each other for a time. After tempers cool and people can relate in a calmer way again, families may find a renewed opportunity to grow in their love and appreciation for one another.

These efforts are last resorts and should not happen the first time there is evidence of a problem. A great deal of energy can go into learning how to resolve the problem, as well as learning new ways to relate, before separation is tried.

Sometimes we as parents may feel stretched to the limit. It may take all of the commitment, love, communication, and tears that we can muster to make our families function. But we need never regret these efforts, for we will have made an investment not only in our own personal well-being, but that of our children.

Next Steps

1. Determine if counseling would be helpful for your family at this time. Do a "counselor search," using referrals you get from family, friends, or other acquaintances, as well as the Yellow Pages of your telephone directory.

2. Identify at least one learning opportunity you could use to enhance your family life—a book you will read, or an enrichment workshop you will attend. If you have trouble finding such workshops, you could encourage your church, school, or other group to sponsor such a series.

12

A Final Word

The goal of all of our efforts toward growth and change is a balance among various elements which mark the healthy family:

• a deep sense of commitment that bonds family members while encouraging individuality;

• the use of both quantity and quality time—an important indicator of our values and priorities;

• expressing love and appreciation so as to build healthy self-esteem as well as family togetherness;

• communicating clearly and listening empathetically;

• resolving conflicts successfully;

• sharing values and faith as a foundation for living.

As a family learns to grow in these areas, its relationship will be marked by a vibrant, healthy relational "glow," an unspoken happiness in being part of that family, a genuine acceptance that goes beyond the conflicts and transitions every family faces.

This image of a healthy family is different from the models in television shows like "The Brady Bunch" or "The Waltons." A family like the Brady Bunch gives the impression that every family crisis can be resolved in 24 minutes, with time out for several commercials. Such images or models can cause persons to feel either angry or guilty that their families do not measure up to this standard, which is really quite unrealistic. The Waltons lived a simple life-style, in which long talks on the porch were daily events, and everyone—no matter what age—went to bed at the same time. It's been a long time since that happened in our family!

For most of us, life is more complicated and exhausting. Many issues surface again and again. At some moments, a family may feel that it is actually falling apart, and, like Humpty Dumpty, will never be put back together again.

In order to become healthier families, we need to move beyond a survival mentality, a life-style in which people merely exist from day to day, from crisis to crisis. Instead, we need a life-style in which we set goals for ourselves and our families about what we want to accomplish in our relationships. Such goals will move us toward establishing a structure that is both meaningful and flexible.

We also need to make our family relationships a priority—not only with our words, but with our calendars, our use of time, and our expenditure of money. Such values will be constantly challenged, since there are many other priorities that can sap our time and financial resources. But our efforts to grow healthy families will lead us to a deeper level of enjoyment and satisfaction that is not found in some of the alternatives in life.

Perhaps you grew up in a family that was—and may now be—dysfunctional. You may find yourself being "hooked" by these dynamics and may feel powerless to overcome some of these difficulties. Or the poor modeling that your parents provided may leave you perplexed as to how to communicate, listen, or show appreciation.

Remember that you do not need to repeat these dysfunctions in your current family. You can choose to change your reaction to any dysfunctions that are still apparent. This may require some counseling, or at least a great deal of effort on your part, but your work will be well worth it. You cannot change the other family members, but you can change your reaction to them and "unhook" from anything that is stifling your own growth.

Perhaps you are in a family situation which feels dysfunctional, a time in which life is quite uncomfortable or tense with your children or spouse. It is amazing how families tend to keep their communication and emotional patterns going, however negative these patterns may be. Some even feel uncomfortable when life begins to go rather well.

A family can choose to change these patterns. Every family member may not be equally enthusiastic, because patterns that have existed will seem comfortable. Change is scary, because it brings us into the unknown and untried. But in order for a family to be healthy, change is often essential.

Every one of our families has areas that can be strengthened and skills that can be sharpened. There seems to be no such thing as the perfect family, in which reactions to problems are marked consistently by maturity, love, and objectivity. Most of us as parents at least occasionally lose control of our tempers or fail to affirm what is positive in our families. Our schedules get off balance, and we spend too much time in our jobs or other outside involvements. Perhaps we do not take the time or know how to communicate effectively.

Becoming a healthy family may require much energy and effort. Like a person's individual growth, there is an ebb and flow to family functioning. There may be periods of relative calm and predictability, followed by transitions or changes that can bring uncertainty, conflict, and turmoil. During these times of change—often when individuals are going through personal changes (like entering school, becoming an adolescent, leaving home, or a midlife transition)—reverberations are felt in the family relationship.

I firmly believe that any effort we make at growing healthy families will be a contribution not only to our personal happiness, but also for the well-being of generations to come. In our generation we have the potential to stop dysfunctions that may have been evident for generations by replacing them with patterns and values marked by love, caring, and commitment.

Lois Duncan has stated it graphically when she described love between the generations as an "ever-growing plant, whose roots, sunk deep into the rich soil of the past, provide the nourishment for tomorrow's blossoms."

For Further Reading

Although I have focused in this book on family health, I have provided some key resources for marriage as well, since the two areas overlap and influence each other a great deal.

Family Health

Ardell, Donald B. *High Level Wellness*. New York: Bantam Books, 1977.

Curran, Dolores. *Traits of a Healthy Family*. Minneapolis: Winston, 1983.

Lewis, Jerry; Beaver, W. Robert; Gossett, John T.; and Phillips, Virginia Austin. *No Single Thread: Psychological Health in Family Systems*. New York: Brunner/Mazel, Publishers, 1976.

Lewis, Jerry M. *How's Your Family? A Guide to Identifying Your Family's Strengths and Weaknesses*. New York: Brunner/Mazel, 1979.

Olson, David H., and Hamilton I. McCubbin & Associates. *Families: What Makes Them Work*. Beverly Hills, Calif.: Sage Publications, 1983.

Sheek, G. William. *A Nation for Families*. Washington, D.C.: American Home Economics Association, 1984.

Stinnett, Nick; Chesser, Barbara; and DeFrain, John; eds. *Building Family Strengths: Blueprints for Action*. Lincoln, Neb.: University of Nebraska Press, 1979.

_____ , eds. *Family Strengths: Positive Models for Family Life*. Lincoln, Neb.: University of Nebraska Press, 1980.

Marriage

Augsburger, David. *Caring Enough to Confront*. Ventura, Calif.: Regal, 1982.

Hunt, Joan, and Hunt, Richard. *Growing Love in Christian Marriage*. Nashville: United Methodist Publishing House, 1981.

Mace, David R. *Success in Marriage*. Nashville: Abingdon, 1980.

Miller, Sherod; Nunnally, Elam W.; and Wackman, Daniel B. *Talking Together: Couple Communication*. Minneapolis: Interpersonal Communication Programs, 1979.

Rubin, Lillian. *Intimate Strangers: Men and Women Together*. New York: Harper & Row, 1983.

Schwartz, Rosly, and Schwartz, Leonard J. *Becoming a Couple: Making the Most of Every Stage of Your Relationship*. Englewood Cliffs, N.J.: Prentice-Hall, 1980.

Tournier, Paul. *To Understand Each Other*. Richmond, Va.: John Knox, 1967.

Divorce, Remarriage, and Stepparenting

Adam, John H., and Adam, Nancy. *Divorce: How and When to Let Go*. Englewood Cliffs, N.J.: Prentice-Hall, 1979.

Block, Joel D. *To Marry Again*. New York: Grosset & Dunlap, 1979.

Berman, Claire. *Making It as a Stepparent*. Garden City, N.Y.: Doubleday, 1980.

Duberman, Lucille. *The Reconstituted Family*. Chicago: Nelson-Hall, 1975.

Duncan, T. Bert, and Duncan, Darlene. *You're Divorced, but Your Children Aren't*. Englewood Cliffs, N.J.: Prentice-Hall, 1979.

Reed, Bobbie. *Stepfamilies: Living in Christian Harmony*. St. Louis, Mo.: Concordia, 1980.

Smoke, Jim. *Suddenly Single.* Old Tappan, N.J.: Fleming H. Revell, 1982.

Visher, Emily, and Visher, John. *Stepfamilies.* New York: Brunner/Mazel, 1979.

Wallenstein, Judith, and Kelly, Joan. *Surviving the Breakup: How Children and Parents Cope with Divorce.* New York: Basic Books, 1980.

Parenting

Bell, Ruth, and Wildflower, Levi. *Talking with Your Teenagers.* New York: Random House, 1983.

Briggs, Dorothy Corkille. *Your Child's Self-Esteem.* Garden City, N.Y.: Doubleday, 1970.

Buth, Lenore. *Sexuality.* St. Louis, Mo.: Concordia, 1983.

Calderone, Mary, and Johnson, Eric. *The Family Book about Sexuality.* New York: Harper and Row, 1981.

Calderone, Mary, and Rammey, James. *Talking with Your Child about Sex.* New York: Delacorte Press, 1979.

Dinkmeyer, Don, and McKay, Gary D. *Systematic Training for Effective Parenting.* Circle Pines, Minn.: American Guidance Service, 1976.

——————— . *Systematic Training for Effective Parenting of Teens.* Circle Pines, Minn.: American Guidance Service, 1984.

Gordon, Sol, and Gordon, Judith. *Raising a Child Conservatively in a Sexually Permissive World.* New York: Simon & Schuster, 1983.

Gow, Kathleen. *Yes, Virginia, There Is Right and Wrong.* New York: John Wiley and Sons, 1980.

Ketterman, Grace, and Ketterman, Herbert L. *The Complete Book of Baby and Child Care for Christian Parents.* Old Tappan, N.J.: Fleming H. Revell, 1982.

Larson, Jim. *Rights, Wrongs, and In-Betweens: Guiding Our Children to Christian Maturity.* Minneapolis: Augsburg, 1984.

Lerman, Saf. *Parent Awareness.* Minneapolis: Winston, 1980.

——————— . *Responsive Parenting.* Circle Pines, Minn.: American Guidance Service, 1984.

McGinnis, Kathleen, and McGinnis, James. *Parenting for Peace and Justice*. Maryknoll, N.Y.: Orbis Books, 1981.

Miller, Mary Susan. *Child-Stress!* Garden City, N.Y.: Doubleday, 1982.

Oraker, James. *Almost Grown: A Christian Guide for Parents of Teenagers*. San Francisco: Harper & Row, 1980.

Rogers, Fred, and Neal, Barry. *Mister Rogers Talks with Parents*. New York: Berkley Books, 1983.

Satir, Virginia. *Peoplemaking*. Palo Alto, Calif.: Science and Behavior Books, 1972.

Scanzoni, Letha. *Sex Is a Parent Affair*. 2nd ed. New York: Bantam, 1982.

Stonehouse, Catherine. *Patterns in Moral Development*. Waco: Word, 1980.

Swihart, Judson, *How to Treat Your Family as Well as You Treat Your Friends*. Ventura, Calif.: Regal, 1982.

Uslander, Arlene S.; Weiss, Caroline; and Telman, Judith. *Sex Education for Today's Child*. New York: Association Press, 1977.

Ward, Ted. *Values Begin at Home*. Wheaton: Victor, 1979.

Westerhoff, John H. *Bringing Up Children in the Christian Faith*. Minneapolis: Winston, 1980.

Resources for Families

Bruisius, Ron, and Noettl, Margaret. *Family Evening Activity Devotions*. St. Louis, Mo.: Concordia, 1980.

Jenkins, Jeanne, and Macdonald, Pam. *Growing Up Equal*. Englewood Cliffs, N.J.: Prentice-Hall, 1979.

Rogers, Fred. *Many Ways to Say I Love You*. Valley Forge, Pa.: Judson, 1977.

Shephard, Mary, and Shephard, Ray. *Vegetable Soup Activities*. New York: Citation, 1975.

Wilt, Joy. *Can-Make-and-Do* series. Waco, Tex.: Word, 1978.

DATE DUE